How To Study Your Bible

Mining the Treasures of God's Word

Rev. Michael Dorsey

Volume 1 of the How To Live series

This book is part of the How To Live series:

How To Study Your Bible
Mining the Treasures of God's Word

ISBN 978-0-9916205-4-8

Copyright © 2016 by Robert Michael Dorsey

Published by Malakim Press
PO Box 456
Aberdeen, MD 21001

Cover art and design by Rose Watters

Cover photo and back cover photo by Jamal Lawson - http://jamallawson.com

This book is dedicated
to my parents...

Robert and Carolyn Dorsey

Thanks for letting me keep
all those books that I
"borrowed" when I left home
to go to Bible school.

Acknowledgements

I would like to thank...

My wife Katherine for pushing me to get
this project finished, but always in her gentle
way, never nagging or criticizing. I love you.

Ted, Dan, Jess, and Carolyn for your
great assistance with editing. Thank
you for making me look smarter.

George, April, and Katherine for sharing such
thought-provoking questions. Thank you.

Pastor Jason Evans and the other ministers
and congregation of Riverside Church for your
genuine love and endless encouragement.

Thank you all so very much.

Read This First!

Each chapter of *How To Study Your Bible* has been divided into 3 sections:

Bible Background - Information about your Bible and where it came from

Bible Study Tools - Resources that will help you get the most out of your Bible

Bible Study Methods - Different ways to explore and learn about your Bible

In the later chapters of the book, brand new Bible students may find the Bible Background section to be a little bit overwhelming because so much information is presented.

Don't let yourself get hung up there!

If you feel like you're starting to get lost, just continue reading the Bible Study Tools and the Bible Study Methods, and go back to the Bible Background sections when you are ready.

Table of Contents

Foreword

I am delighted to have been offered the opportunity to comment on the profound practicality of this work by Brother Dorsey. For those who have had the privilege to sit under his teaching or read one of his books, you know that this work is distinctly "Brother Michael." He is one of a few Theological teachers who are able to make the unpalatable palatable and the incomprehensible comprehensible.

From the seminary student to the John Doe Christian, all will be greatly helped and enlightened by this work that serves as a study guide as well as a personal companion resource.

I personally found this work exceptionally clear, quite easy to understand, and necessary in the church to help disciple saints in developing a basic, solid foundation for the balance of their Christian lives. From understanding the origin of our Bible to discovering how it was translated into our language through the power of the Holy Spirit, he has made it both interesting and informative.

This is a must-read for pastors and a must-have as a discipleship study.

Thanks, Brother Dorsey, for a work so spiritually crafted and obediently written.

Pastor James E. Morris, Sr.
Christ-Anointed Church
Jackson, Mississippi

Introduction

*How can a young person
stay on the path of purity?
By living according to your
word. - Psalm 119:9 (NIV)*

The Bible is the most amazing book ever written, but for too many Christians its contents are a mystery. I didn't realize this early on in my Christian life. I was raised going to Sunday school every week at 9:30 AM, right before the 11 AM church service. So naturally, as I was growing up, I thought everybody in America knew who Abraham, Moses, David, Peter, and Paul were, but I've come to learn that's not the case.

Riverside Church, where I attend (I'm not the Pastor), has seen incredible growth over the past few years, and most of our new attendees are not church transplants from other denominations. For the vast majority of these people, their spiritual background was "sinner."

The great thing about that is they're not carrying very much religious baggage. They don't have any Pharisaic legalism or unscriptural religious traditions they need to unlearn, which is great. However, the downside is they know next to nothing about the Word of God.

If you grew up being taught about the Bible, as I was, it may be difficult for you to understand what a new convert faces when she starts her Christian walk. One of the first things we tell her to do is to start reading her Bible, and so she goes out and buys herself a copy.

When she opens it and starts reading, she realizes she doesn't understand a lot of what she's reading. The Bible is a thick book of tiny print on very thin pages with hardly any pictures. It can be very intimidating to a new believer!

Then she finds there are all these different books inside. Where should she start? What should she read first? Which part should she read next? Should she try to read the books of the Bible in order? Are some sections more relevant than others?

She also learns there are different versions of the Bible. What's the deal with that? Are some versions better than others? Are certain translations more reliable? How can she decide which one she should choose?

Not wanting to look foolish, she doesn't ask anyone these questions, lest she be embarrassed. Instead, she just soldiers on as best she can, learning things here and there as she's able. After a few years she's a faithful church goer, yet while she's been able to pick up a few things along the way, the Bible largely remains a mystery to her.

I've learned this is just about exactly where most people are today. Revival is spreading across this nation, and many who never thought they'd consider God as a factor in their lives have received Jesus Christ as their Lord and Savior. As these people come into the Kingdom, there is a tremendous need for them to be instructed in the Word of God.

Then there are so many "older" Christians who also know very little about their Bible. Part of the problem is that Spirit-filled worship sometimes places a greater emphasis on spiritual experiences than it does on the effort of studying and learning the written Word of God.

Another part of the problem is there are so few who are truly capable of teaching the Word to God's people, and even fewer opportunities for them to do so in today's church culture. Unfortunately, the church overall hasn't made the necessary effort to help Christians become proficient in the use of their Bibles. However, I believe that's about to change.

Because you're holding this book in your hand, that tells me you are hungry to learn more about your Bible, how to study it, and how to use it. You're a believer in Jesus Christ. Now you want to grow up spiritually and stand on your own, no longer having to be overly dependent on others when it comes to understanding the Word of God.

You're the reason things are about to change. Your desire to be spiritually equipped, in order to not be tossed about by every wind of doctrine that blows past, is the reason God has placed *How To Study Your Bible* in your hands.

This book began as a 4-week course I taught at

Riverside Church in the summer of 2013. As soon as everyone who was able to attend realized they were about to be informed and empowered on how to study the Bible for themselves, their excitement spread like wildfire.

Of course, as a Bible teacher, I was hoping they would become inspired as they began to see the new potential reality that was unfolding before them, but their enthusiasm surprised even me. I still thank God for that, and give Him all of the glory, because I know it's only by His Word, through faith in His Word, that lives are changed.

Since there hasn't been an opportunity for me to teach that class again, and because many have asked me when the course will be repeated, the Spirit of God led me to create this book from that material. My brothers and sisters at church were excited when they heard about this book, and even more so when they discovered it would contain everything that was taught in the original 4-week course, plus much more.

Likewise, I'm very excited because I know this material has the potential to reach a thousand times more people in book format than I could reach by teaching the course again, even if I were to teach it 12 months out of the year.

After watching what God did in the lives of those who were able to go through the original lessons with me, I can't wait to see what He's about to do in the lives of His people as this book becomes widely distributed.

In the original course, we covered information

about the Bible, Bible study tools, and Bible study methods. The students also did hands-on exercises during the class to learn the various different Bible study methods. In order to help keep things interesting in the class, I decided to mix things up a little.

We didn't cover all of the information about the Bible at the beginning of the course and then cram in all the different Bible study methods at the end. Instead, each class started by talking about some different aspect of the Bible. Then some new Bible study tools were introduced, and finally some new Bible study methods were presented, along with targeted exercises to practice those new methods that had just been discussed.

That worked so well when I taught the course that I've structured this book the same way. At the beginning of each chapter I will teach you something new about the Bible, then cover some of the best Bible study tools that are available, and we'll end each chapter by introducing a new Bible study method. For practice exercises, I encourage you to get a copy of *Sword Drills,* the companion workbook for *How To Study Your Bible.*

At the close of each chapter you'll also find discussion questions which are ideal for weekly study groups. Small groups are encouraged to practice some of the Bible study methods when meeting together. Usually, individuals will approach each method slightly differently, so the group as a whole will benefit from the various perspectives of its different members.

By the time you've finished reading this book, not

only will you no longer be intimidated by the Bible, but you'll be fully equipped with a new spiritual tool belt that will enable you to mine the Word of God for nuggets of revelation that you can then easily apply to your own life.

One other note about this book: I have exerted no effort whatsoever to insure that the male and female genders are both included at all times. At times I will refer to "he" and "him," and in other places I will refer to "she" and "her." Obviously, either applies and one could easily be substituted for the other in those places.

Let me close with a personal thought. I'm known as a "Bible guru" at my church, and have sometimes even been referred to as a "Bible scholar." To be honest, I really don't care for those titles.

I appreciate the compliment as intended, but the problem is it places me high up on a spiritual pedestal, while implying that others who are supposedly "below" me really have no hope of reaching that higher level themselves.

Instead, I much prefer to be called a Bible *student* because that's really what I am, but more importantly because that's what YOU can become too! As a student of the Bible, my sincere hope is that you'll catch up to the place that I've been able to attain, and hopefully even pass me someday. Why not?

You can do it, Bible student. You just need someone to show you the way! With greater understanding will come greater comfort with the Bible. With greater comfort will come greater enthusiasm, and with greater enthusiasm will come greater proficiency at Bible study.

Once you become proficient at Bible study, God will bless your determination with fresh revelation from the treasure of His Word. As you set out to learn *How To Study Your Bible,* I hope you're excited. I'm excited for you!

Michael Dorsey

August 2016

Chapter 1

Where Do I Begin?

Getting Started with Your Bible

*All Scripture is given by inspiration
of God, and is profitable for
doctrine, for reproof, for correction,
for instruction in righteousness:
- 2 Timothy 3:16 (KJV)*

The Bible is unlike any other book in the world. It is a masterpiece of ancient literature and the best-selling book of all time, yet it is so much more than that. It is the written Word of God, and that makes the Bible a living book. By "living," I don't mean a book that's constantly in development and changing. What I mean is the book is spiritually alive.

For the word of God is living and active, sharper than any two-edged sword, piercing to the division of soul and of spirit, of joints and of marrow, and discerning the thoughts and intentions of the heart. - Hebrews 4:12

One of the characteristics of living things is that they interact with each other, and without a doubt this book will interact with your spirit if you allow it to. The living, active

Word will cut into you more efficiently than any blade ever could, surgically revealing the thoughts and intents of your heart.

Why is this holy book able to do this? How is it possible that simply exposing ourselves to it can affect us so deeply? What is it about the Bible that makes it different from any other book in the world? The answer is simple: The writings of the Bible were inspired by the Holy Spirit of God.

Inspiration Defined

The Bible says that all Scripture was given by inspiration of God (2 Timothy 3:16). The word "inspired" is related to the word "respiration." It literally means "God-breathed," and more modern translations such as the English Standard Version render it so:

All Scripture is breathed out by God and profitable for teaching, for reproof, for correction, and for training in righteousness:
- 2 Timothy 3:16

Most denominational statements of faith include the belief that all Scripture is inspired by God, but what's the meaning behind that? We know the various books of the Bible were written by human authors, yet we also know that all men, including the Biblical writers, are sinners by nature (Romans 3:23). So how did the act of inspiration actually happen? Did God take control of the Bible's authors, possessing them and forcing them to record His words through some sort of automatic writing?

For prophecy never came by the will of man, but holy men of God spoke as they were moved by the Holy Spirit. - 2 Peter 1:21 (NKJ)

No, holy men wrote as the Holy Spirit moved them when "the word of the Lord" came to them. While these human authors chose the words that reflected their style, personality, language, culture, and circumstances, God guided the process so each word would convey His message accurately. In other words, God's power enabled these men to correctly record the truth He revealed to them.

As a result of divine inspiration, the Bible is the sole authority for doctrine and the infallible rule of faith for Christian living. We can rely on the Word of God, and that allows us to feel secure in making it the foundation of our lives, because God is faithful to His Word.

Heaven and earth will pass away, but my words will never pass away. - Matthew 24:35 (NIV)

This inspiration of Scripture includes both the Old and New Testaments. Jesus referred to many Old Testament persons and events, and in doing so, He bore testimony to the authenticity and the authority of the Old Testament. The words of Paul in II Timothy 3:16 (quoted at the start of this chapter) might also be viewed as having reference only to the Old Testament, since the New Testament was still in the process of being written then.

However, the writings of the Apostles, including Paul and certain others, were also recognized early on as Scripture. This is apparent from the words of Peter:

And count the patience of our Lord as salvation, just as our beloved brother Paul also wrote to you according to the wisdom given him, as he does in all his letters when he speaks in them of these matters. There are some things in them that are hard to understand, which the ignorant and unstable twist to their own destruction, AS THEY DO THE OTHER SCRIPTURES.
- 2 Peter 3:15, 16

Although Peter refers here to Paul's writings as Scripture, notice how he also points out that parts of Paul's writings can be hard to understand. This is an important point regarding inspiration: One can believe in the inspiration of the Bible despite having not yet attained a full and complete understanding of the Scriptures. The key factor is faith in God's Word, not intellectual understanding.

And we also thank God constantly for this, that when you received the word of God, which you heard from us, you accepted it not as the word of men but as what it really is, the word of God, which is at work in you believers.
- 1 Thessalonians 2:13

When we acknowledge that Scripture is divinely inspired, we can then rely on it as the basis and foundation for our entire life. As a Christian you will at times come across teachings or accounts of supernatural experiences that will seem questionable to you. How can you tell whether a certain teaching or spiritual experience is valid or not?

This is what we mean when we say the Bible is authoritative. The God who "breathed" the Scriptures in the first place is the same Holy Spirit who is at work in the church today. That means any so-called new revelation, or any claim of a supernatural vision or similar spiritual experience, must always be measured against the written Word of God. When issues like these arise, our first question must always be, "What does the Bible say?"

Without the authority of holy Scripture, truth will soon be compounded by error because of human fallibility. When people claim they are sharing divine revelation, whether it sounds questionable to you or even if it sounds good to you, your first questions should always be, "Can you please point that out to me in the Bible? Would you show me the Scripture for that?"

I don't care who they are, if they can't show me their "revelation" in the Word of God, then I won't receive it. Too many Christians are like the Athenians in the Book of Acts, spending all of their time trying to find a new revelation, seeking out some new truth that no one else has ever heard before.

Now all the Athenians and the foreigners who lived there would spend their time in nothing except telling or hearing something new.
- Acts 17:21

Instead, we need to be more like the Bereans, who were Christians that Paul commended for giving primacy to the written Word of God, and for honoring the Scriptures as authoritative:

The brothers immediately sent Paul and Silas away by night to Berea, and when they arrived they went into the Jewish synagogue. Now these Jews were more noble than those in Thessalonica; they received the word with all eagerness, examining the Scriptures daily to see if these things were so. - Acts 17:10, 11

The concept of the divine inspiration is critically important as we continue learning how to study the Bible. You will be able to identify whether something is scriptural or not only to the extent that you actually know the Scriptures. That's why learning how to study the Bible is so important to your Christian life, even more important than learning how to pray.

If one turns away his ear from hearing the law (the Word), **even his prayer is an abomination.** **- Proverbs 28:9**

Our prayers must be based on the Word of God or they won't work. Everything in our lives should be based on the Bible. It is the only sure foundation that we can build our lives upon, but to get the most benefit out of these Scriptures God has given us, we have to find out what is in them.

By recognizing that God breathed out the Scriptures that were then recorded faithfully by holy men of God, you can feel safe in basing not only your theology but your entire life on the written Word. Errors may sometimes arise in copying, translating, or printing the Scriptures, but God has kept his hand on the transmission process to preserve His Word for all time.

> **For the Lord is good;**
> **His mercy is everlasting,**
> **And His truth endures to all generations.**
> **- Psalms 100:5 (NKJ)**

Bible Study Tools #1
Your Own Bible

The most important tool for Bible study is your very own Bible. I know that sounds obvious and maybe even a little bit simplistic, but when you look into it a little bit deeper it's actually a very profound statement. Notice I didn't say "the Bible," but rather, "your Bible."

Later in this book we'll look at specific study Bibles and answer questions such as, "What Bible version should I use?" That's not what I'm talking about here. You need to find a Bible that you're comfortable with, one that feels good in your hands when you're using it.

In the Bible, the Word of God is compared to a sword, an illustration that means God's Word is like a weapon in the spirit realm (Hebrews 4:12, Ephesians 6:17). Just as a steel sword is a weapon in the natural realm, so the sword of the Spirit is a critically important piece of equipment in your spiritual warfare kit.

I remember watching a documentary on television about the making of the *Lord of the Rings* movies. They were interviewing Viggo Mortensen about his role as Aragorn in the films, and they were focusing on how he had to be trained to sword fight. They went into great detail about how a personal trainer was hired for him, both to build up his strength and to teach him how to use his sword safely.

If you've ever held a real sword, you know how odd they can feel. The documentary also made the point about how every sword is different, each with its own idiosyncrasies. While a man might be trained to use swords in general, over time he will become more accustomed to the one he uses most often, and if he holds a different sword it will actually feel different and a little bit weird to him.

While I was watching this, I realized that we're exactly the same way with our spiritual swords. You'll grow used to the Bible that you use all the time. You may not know exactly where a specific Scripture verse is located in your Bible, but you'll remember that it's in the middle of the New Testament, on the lower half of the first column on the left-hand page, and you'll be able to find it in less than a minute.

Yet, when you're "holding someone else's sword," looking for the very same verse in their Bible, it's almost as if you have an entirely different book in your hands. You're not used to it. Now of course, it would be best if you were eventually able to memorize the Scripture reference so you could find it in any Bible, but most believers don't start there, do they? No, they get used to their Bible because it's theirs. It's the sword they train on all the time.

That's why it's so important to find a Bible that you like, and even more so, one that you can use, and one that you *will* use. I don't have anything against giant decorative Bibles on the coffee table or cherishing a Bible that was given to you on some special occasion. I have a Bible that belonged to my Grandpa Dennis, and it's one of my most prized possessions. I don't use it for reading or studying because it's old and fragile, but also because I know it would be awkward for me if I did try to use it that way.

I have other Bibles though, and one in particular that I use every day. This is my main sword. It has a soft leather cover, but it's durable. I can hold it easily in one hand, the print isn't too small, and it's a version that's easy to read. Also, there aren't a lot of extra notes and other material on the pages, just the Bible verses and a small center-column reference. It works for me, and I like it.

You need to find a Bible that will work for you, a sword that feels right in your hands when you swing it at the enemy. By the time you get to the end of this book you'll have a much clearer picture of the kind of Bible you should get. You'll probably end up using several Bibles, with one Bible for devotional reading and carrying to church, and other Bibles for serious in-depth study.

If you don't have any idea what to look for, don't worry about it. If you already have a Bible, you can get started with that for now. As you continue reading, you'll learn more about what to look for in a good Bible. Start thinking about it now, though, because the #1 most important Bible study tool you'll ever have or use is your own everyday Bible.

Bible Study Method #1
Devotional Bible Reading

Devotional Bible reading simply means devoting yourself to reading a portion of the Scriptures each day. One reason why you need to find a Bible that you really enjoy using is because you'll be reading it every day during your devotional time. Now, when we talk about daily devotional reading, what does that involve?

Over the years I've talked to many believers who were struggling with different kinds of problems. Some were tormented by evil thoughts. Others had a sickness in their body or were fighting some sort of addiction. Still others were being challenged by a set of negative circumstances that had suddenly and unexpectedly appeared, and their faith was being stretched. Yet they all seemed to have one thing in common: They were looking for a magic bullet to help them out of their problem.

Too often Christians think they can come to the altar to get "zapped" by the minister laying hands on them, or they can just utter some formulaic confession, and their problems will be solved. When that doesn't happen, they come to me looking for answers. They want to know what they need to do to escape their troubles, and they think I can help them. They believe there's some hidden knowledge or secret revelation that will help them if I would only reveal it to them.

So I give them my best answer: "Let me tell you the one thing, above anything else, that has helped me spiritually.

What I'm about to share with you has, without a doubt, been the key to my spiritual growth and to achieving stability in my life. Here it is..." At this point they're leaning in close, waiting to hear the rest of the answer.

I tell them, "The one thing that has benefitted me above all else in my walk with God is this: consistent daily Bible reading and prayer." When they hear this, their head drops and they let out a heavy sigh, because they wanted some obscure secret that would magically solve everything, and that wasn't the answer they were looking for. It may not be the answer you were looking for either, but it's still the answer.

Consistency Is The Key

When trouble comes your way, there is nothing that will fortify your spirit and strengthen your heart like reading the Word and spending time in the presence of your Heavenly Father on a daily basis. However, for some reason a lot of Christians can't seem to accept that. They think it has to somehow be more difficult than that, or that the answer has to be more intricate and complex.

In 2 Kings chapter 5, Naaman, the famous Syrian general, comes to the prophet Elijah to seek healing for his leprosy. Elijah doesn't even come out to speak with him, but rather sends his servant to instruct him to go wash in the dirty Jordan River seven times. Naaman is outraged and insulted, telling the servant that there are beautiful, clear rivers in Assyria that he could wash in, and he leaves there without being healed.

However, Naaman was blessed to have some men with him who cared for him and were very wise:

> **But his officers tried to reason with him and said, "Sir, if the prophet had told you to do something very difficult, wouldn't you have done it? So you should certainly obey him when he says simply, 'Go and wash and be cured!'"**
> **- 2 Kings 5:13 (NLT)**

Naaman realized his men were right, he obeyed the prophet's simple instructions, and he finally received his healing, but at first he had a lot of trouble with the simplicity of God's solution for his problem. Many Christians are the same way.

It reminds me of the New Year's resolutions people make every year to get into shape. They're fired up at first, and they hit the gym and work out for several hours every day. This lasts for only a couple of weeks, and then they don't show up at the gym as often, and after a couple of months they aren't there at all. It would have been so much better if they'd just exercised at home for 20-30 minutes per day, and done so consistently, day after day.

Spiritual exercise works the same way. Too often Christians will become convicted in their hearts by their lack of Bible reading, and they will start trying to read and study for 3 hours a day. That's like sitting down at the bench press and trying to start out pushing 400 lbs. of weights. It would be so much better, and so much more productive, if they would just read a little bit in their Bible each day, and do it consistently, each and every day.

Expose Yourself to the Word

Another reason daily devotional reading is so important is because of what we said at the beginning of the chapter: The Word of God is alive!

For the word of God is living and active, sharper than any two-edged sword, piercing to the division of soul and of spirit, of joints and of marrow, and discerning the thoughts and intentions of the heart. - Hebrews 4:12

The best example I can think of to illustrate this is a negative example, but it does get the point across. Let's say you were to find a ball of uranium-238, and you put it in your pocket and forgot about it. As the days and weeks passed, that radioactive material would start to change you. Your cellular structure would begin to disintegrate, and in less than three weeks you'd most likely be dead, all because of the changes your body experienced due to its close exposure to that uranium.

The Bible works the same way in your spirit, but in a positive direction. You can't help but be changed on the inside when you're exposed to the light of the living Word, and the more you're exposed, the more you'll change and grow for the better.

The power of devotional reading isn't found in the development of a holy habit of daily Bible reading. Although that's certainly not a bad thing, the true essence of daily devotional reading is the exposure of your spirit to the life of God that is contained in His Word. That's what devotional reading is all about, and when you come to that realization, then the prospect of reading your Bible every day will seem a lot less tedious.

Devotional reading isn't technically a method of Bible study per se. You will come across things during your devotional reading that interest you, topics which you may decide to study out later, but the purpose of your devotional reading time isn't to study.

If you're a preacher or Bible teacher, you have to be especially careful about this. Your temptation will be to study during your daily devotions, and you'll wind up using that time coming up with material to benefit your people, when devotional reading is really intended for your own personal benefit.

Just because you may be a great cook, that doesn't mean you don't need to also eat food yourself. Daily devotional Bible reading is a necessary foundation for your Christian life, and it will position you to get the most out of the other methods of Bible study that are covered later in this book.

Devotional Reading – A How-To Guide

If you've never done consistent devotional reading before, you're going to want to start small. You don't want to set a goal that's too ambitious, and you can always add more reading later when you're ready. I suggest you begin with the New Testament, reading one chapter per day. If you read one chapter each day, Monday through Friday, you will read through the entire New Testament in one year.

Devotional reading is typically done by yourself. Doing it alone will help to prevent you from being distracted while you're reading, because News Flash: The devil does not want you doing this. You also might want to set up a time for family devotional reading, to help teach your children the habit of daily Bible reading. However, you should still do your personal devotion time alone so you can focus on the Lord.

It's also best if you can read your daily chapter out loud, at least loud enough that you're able to hear it with your own ears. Why is that important? Because the Bible says that "...faith comes by hearing, and hearing by the Word of God." (Romans 10:17). There's a benefit in hearing the Word with your own ears, from your own voice.

If you're not that great of a reader, don't worry about it. Just do the best you can. Smith Wigglesworth was an uneducated, illiterate plumber when he came to the Lord, but after he got saved he was able to read his Bible. That's also another reason why it's a good idea to do your devotional reading alone – everybody gets tripped up on those long Bible names!

Eventually you'll get to a place where you're still spiritually "hungry" after reading your one chapter. That's when you'll know it's time to add more. I suggest adding the Book of Proverbs next. It's full of short one-liners of truth, and there are 31 chapters, one for each day of the month. You can read the 1st chapter on the 1st day of the month, the 2nd chapter the next day, and so on. Later you can add more.

Just remember, the biggest key is consistency. If you miss a day, don't beat yourself up over it. Just pick up where you were on the following day. Don't try to read ahead or play "catch up" at the end of the week. Just make the time to read at least one chapter each day, and allow God to speak to you through His holy Word.

Summary

The divine inspiration of the Bible is the foundation for your ability to understand the Scriptures, as well as the basis of all of the Bible study methods that you're going to learn in this book. Because the Bible is inspired, it is the infallible Word of God in all matters of faith and practice, and we should recognize the written Word as authoritative in our lives.

When we do so, we position ourselves by faith to receive further revelation and understanding of the Word through the ministry of the Holy Spirit. We also protect ourselves from deception. Any time some supposedly new Christian teaching, or someone's testimony of an alleged spiritual experience, comes across our path, our first response should always be, "Show me the Scripture."

This principle inevitably leads us to the fact that we must know the Bible for ourselves, and a key factor in doing so is finding a Bible that we feel comfortable using every day. Just as a swordsman who is trained to use all swords will be the most proficient with his own, so will you be most effective with the Bible that you use most often.

That means you need to find a Bible that you like, and you must eventually decide which translation you will use. You don't want to overlook things such as how it feels in your hands, or how easy it is to read the print. Since you're going to be using your Bible every day, you certainly don't want to be stuck with one that annoys you for any reason.

Having understood the implications of divine inspiration on the Bible's authority in all matters of faith and life, and having obtained a Bible that you're comfortable using, the next step is to simply begin exposing yourself to the life of the Word of God by taking it in every day. This is done through devotional reading.

Devotional Bible reading involves establishing a daily habit of Bible reading that you stick to on a consistent basis. You can start out by reading just one chapter a day. It doesn't really matter where you start reading, or how much you read in one sitting, because if it's in the Bible it will be of benefit to you spiritually, even if you don't fully understand what you're reading at first. The key is to do it consistently, every day.

Now that we've looked at how to get started with your Bible, you need to start getting more familiar with it. That begins by getting an overview of this amazing book, along with a few more steps that will help you get prepared for maximum profitability in your Bible study.

Chapter 1 Discussion Questions

1. How can we base our modern life on a document over 2000 years old, written before all of our technological advances? What parts of the Bible remain constant?

2. Why should The Holy Bible be the absolute authority on Christian life and doctrine (teaching)?

3. How will a broad knowledge of the Bible help you to determine what practices are and are not scriptural?

4. How does The Bible seek to uncover the thoughts and intentions of our hearts?

5. As you read the Bible, you can draw strength and comfort from the Scriptures, even without fully understanding them. Why and how is this possible?

6. What are some unique advantages to having your own, personal everyday-use Bible?

7. From what you've read, what is the principal benefit of a daily devotion?

8. How do you know what devotional goal is reasonable for you? Are you challenged, overloaded, or bored with your daily routine? How long would you strive for a goal before you change it?

9. How will a commitment to daily devotion make other biblical resources (such as this book) more useful to you?

Chapter 2

Looking Through A Wide-Angle Lens

Getting Acquainted With Your Bible

Study and be eager and do your utmost to present yourself to God approved (tested by trial), a workman who has no cause to be ashamed, correctly analyzing and accurately dividing [rightly handling and skillfully teaching] the Word of Truth. - 2 Timothy 2:15 (AMP)

Daily devotional reading is incredibly important, and you have to do it consistently every day to get the most out of it. If you have to choose between your devotional reading time and time spent studying the Bible in other ways, I recommend making the devotional time a priority. It's just too easy to get busy with other things (including good things such as other methods of studying the Bible!) and let your daily devotional time slip away.

With that understanding, however, you also need to set aside time during each week that is dedicated specifically to Bible study. You have to take on the mentality of a Bible student, recognizing that the pursuit of studying the Bible will last for the remainder of your lifetime.

You will never master the entirety of the Word of God, because no matter how far you go there is always another nugget of truth to dig out, another layer of understanding to be reached, and another revelation to be imparted to your spirit. There will be times when you read a passage of Scripture that you've read 100 times, but this time something new will jump out at you.

The Word is alive, and while you should always "study and be eager and do your utmost... correctly and accurately... rightly handling... the Word of truth," the pursuit of mastering the Bible is an adventure that will last a lifetime. That's why it's important to not look at Bible study as an event, but as a mentality that you must adopt and internalize. Let your confession be: "From this day forward, I am a student of the Bible, and the Holy Spirit is my teacher."

Layout of the Bible

The first step in becoming a Bible student is learning how the Bible is laid out. The Bible is actually a "library" of books, containing 66 different books. You probably already know the Scriptures are divided into the Old and New Testaments, sometimes referred to as the Old Covenant and the New Covenant. The Old Testament is made up of 39 books, while the New Testament contains 27 books.

The books in each testament are further subdivided as follows:

Old Testament

The Pentateuch – Genesis, Exodus, Leviticus, Numbers, and Deuteronomy

Pentateuch (pronounced *pent-uh-tewk*) means "five books," and these make up the opening section of the Old Testament. Moses was the author of these books, which contain the origins of creation and the 12 tribes of Israel, as well as details about the Law God gave to Moses for the Israelites to follow.

Historical Books – Joshua, Judges, Ruth, 1 Samuel, 2 Samuel, 1 Kings, 2 Kings, 1 Chronicles, 2 Chronicles, Ezra, Nehemiah, and Esther

These books, written by various authors, continue to tell the story of the nation of Israel. Joshua, Judges, and Ruth cover the conquest of the land of Canaan and the history of the twelve tribes of Israel before the monarchy. First and Second Samuel tell the story of how Israel became a nation ruled by a king.

First and Second Kings cover the dividing of the kingdom into two opposing nations, Israel and Judah, and the reigns of the kings that followed in each nation, up until the captivity period. First and Second Chronicles cover much of the same material related in First and Second Kings, but First and Second Kings tell the story from the Kingdom of Israel's point of view, while First and Second Chronicles cover it from the viewpoint of the Kingdom of Judah.

Eventually, both the Kingdoms of Israel and Judah fell due to their sin. Israel was conquered by the nation of Assyria, and Judah fell to the armies of Babylon. At that time it was the practice of these nations to carry the populations of the people they conquered into captivity. The books of Ezra, Nehemiah, and Esther reflect the period of the Judean captivity in Babylon and their eventual return to the land of Israel when their captivity was over.

Poetry – Job, Psalms, Proverbs, Ecclesiastes, and Song of Solomon

Sometimes referred to as the Wisdom books, this group represents writings that are more poetic in nature. The story of Job is considered to be one of the oldest writings in the world. Psalms contains the lyrics of songs, mostly written by King David, but some were also written by Moses and others. Proverbs, Ecclesiastes, and Song of Solomon were written by King David's son, King Solomon, who is considered the wisest man in the history of the world.

Major Prophets – Isaiah, Jeremiah, Lamentations, Ezekiel, and Daniel

The Prophets were God's spokesmen in the Old Testament. They were the ones who said, "Thus saith the Lord," delivering the messages God had for His people. The writings included in the Major Prophets are of greater length than those of the Minor Prophets, and also cover subjects and events that are of generally greater importance. Each book is named after its author, with Jeremiah also having written Lamentations.

Minor Prophets – Hosea, Joel, Amos, Obadiah, Jonah, Micah, Nahum, Habakkuk, Zephaniah, Haggai, Zechariah, and Malachi

The Minor Prophets, sometimes referred to as the Book of the Twelve because there are 12 of them, are similar to the writings of the Major Prophets, but they are typically much shorter.

These are the pages that are usually stuck together in the back of your Old Testament. The last of the Minor Prophets was the Book of Malachi, after which there was over 400 years of silence as history passed, until the time the next books of the Bible were written.

New Testament

The Gospels – Matthew, Mark, Luke, and John

The four Gospels tell the good news of the birth, life, and ministry of the Lord Jesus Christ, climaxing with His death on the cross, His burial, and His resurrection. Technically speaking, Jesus operated on Earth as a Prophet under the Old Covenant.

Therefore, it could be argued, from a theological standpoint, that the Gospels should be grouped with the Old Testament, since the New Covenant didn't actually begin until Jesus' resurrection. However, since they are historically closer to the rest of the New Testament books, they make up the opening books of the New Testament.

History – Acts

The Book of Acts details the history of the Apostles and the growth of the early church in the years immediately following the ministry of Jesus. The first 12 chapters emphasize the ministry of the Apostle Peter, while the remaining 16 chapters focus on the ministry of the Apostle Paul, especially his missionary journeys throughout the Roman Empire.

Pauline Epistles – Romans, 1 and 2 Corinthians, Galatians, Ephesians, Philippians, Colossians, 1 and 2 Thessalonians, 1 and 2 Timothy, Titus, and Philemon

The word "epistle" means a formal letter, and this group of books consists of letters written by the Apostle Paul. The Pauline Epistles (pronounced paul-line, not paul-leen) can be subdivided into two groups: letters to churches and Pastoral Epistles. The churches that Paul wrote to were those he started or visited during his missionary trips that are detailed in the Book of Acts. For example, the Book of Ephesians was written to the church at Ephesus. The Pastoral Epistles were written to individuals. Timothy and Titus were ministers that Paul mentored, and Philemon was one of his supporters.

General Epistles – Hebrews, James, 1 Peter, 2 Peter, 1 John, 2 John, 3 John, and Jude

The General Epistles are so named because they were written to the entire church in general. The Pauline Epistles were always specifically addressed either to a certain church or to an individual, but the General Epistles were written to the church at large. Except for the Book of Hebrews, the General Epistles are named after their authors, the Apostles Peter and John, and also James and Jude, who were two of Jesus' younger brothers.

It isn't entirely clear who wrote the Book of Hebrews, as the author isn't identified. However, most believe it was probably either Paul, or someone who worked closely with Paul, and the Book of Hebrews should be grouped with the Pauline Epistles (as it was historically). Like the other General Epistles, it was written to all of the Hebrew Christians who were spread out across the Roman Empire.

Prophecy - Revelation

The only prophetic writing of the New Testament, the Book of Revelation, covers God's judgment upon those who rejected His Son, along with the events that will happen at the end of the age. It ends on an encouraging note with the final defeat of God's enemies and the revelation of a new Heaven and Earth.

We will go into more detail about the "story" of the Bible in chapter four, but here we have covered the basic layout of the Bible as we have it today. As a student of the Bible, you will want to eventually memorize this layout, as it will become the foundation for everything else you will learn.

For example, when you're listening to a sermon on Sunday morning and the pastor directs you to the Scripture he will be speaking on, it's very helpful to know whether that passage is in the historical books of the Old Testament, or the writings of the Prophets, or if it's in the Gospels, or one of the epistles written by Paul.

Knowing what part of the Bible the minister is starting from will give you the ability to immediately place the passage within its correct context, and being able to do that will increase the value and meaning of the things that you hear in the message. That is just one of the many advantages of developing a Bible student mentality.

Bible Study Tools #2
A Good Study Space

When we were talking about devotional Bible reading in chapter one, I made the point that Bible reading isn't really the same thing as Bible study. In my book *How To Pray,* I discussed some of the characteristics of a good "prayer closet," and some things you can do to make a room better suited for prayer. That same kind of room, comfortable and free from distractions, would be ideal for your daily devotions, but it probably wouldn't be the best place to do actual Bible study.

An ideal study space is an essential element of quality Bible study, but it's one that's often overlooked. Yet the simple fact is this: If you don't have a good place to do your studying, you're not going to get the full benefit out of your Bible study efforts. Why not stack the odds in your favor by taking just a little bit of time to set up a study desk that works for you?

You'll need to decide where your study desk is going to be. You might have a home office or a desk already set up in your basement or spare bedroom. You may want to use your kitchen table, or set up a study desk in your prayer room as described above. Wherever you decide to put it, there are some things you should consider.

First, will your place of study be available to you whenever you need it? If you can't use it when you need it, then it won't do you much good. If you are using a place that you must share with others, it may be helpful to work out a schedule so that you know when you can use it.

Second, your place of study should be free from interruptions and distractions. Silence your cell phone, close the door, and post a "Do Not Disturb" sign if necessary. Research shows that the best study time is uninterrupted time that is free of distractions. If you like playing music while you study, instrumental music is best with the volume kept low.

Third, does this place have all of the study materials you need? We will be examining many study materials throughout this book, but you already know you'll need pens and pencils, a ruler, and paper or a notebook. If you use a computer for Bible study (which we will also be covering), it should also be accessible from your study area.

Fourth, does your study space have a large enough desk? Now when I say desk, I just mean a place to sit where you can do your studying. It doesn't have to be an expensive, ornate desk. In fact, a four-foot long folding table would do just fine. You don't need to spend a lot of money to create a study space. That money would be better spent on study materials! You just want enough surface space to hold everything you need, without feeling cluttered, even when your materials are all spread out.

Fifth, think about what kind of chair you will be using. An uncomfortable chair can cause discomfort or pain over time, and that will interfere with your studying. A chair that is too comfortable might make you tired. Your posture while studying is also important. When reclining or lying down it's harder to maintain the same level of active concentration as when you are sitting up straight. Select a chair in which you can sit for long periods while maintaining a high level of attention.

Finally, think about your study area's environment. Is there enough light for you to be able to see clearly without any strain or discomfort? What about the temperature? If your place of study becomes too warm, you might get sleepy. If it gets too cold, then your thoughts may slow down and become unclear. Select the temperature at which your body and mind function the best.

This may seem like a lot to consider at one time, but once you set up your study area it's easy to maintain it, and eventually you won't have to think about it all. It will just become second nature to you.

Soon, studying in a strategically structured environment, free from distractions and interruptions, will simply be "the way my studying happens," and you will be well on your way to building your Bible student mentality.

Bible Study Method #2
Survey Studies

This chapter has been about looking at the Bible through a wide-angle lens, and we're going to stick with that theme as we examine our next Bible study method: survey studies. Most survey studies are a survey of either the Old Testament or the New Testament.

If you've ever driven past surveyors who were on the side of the road conducting a survey, you'll have an idea of what a survey study is about. Those surveyors work hard to make sure their measurements are precise, so that the lines on our maps appear in the right places. Thanks to the surveyor's efforts, we can look at a map on which one centimeter may equal one kilometer and get a good bird's-eye view of the landscape. There isn't a lot of detail that we can see, but we're able to get a good idea of the general area.

Survey studies of the Bible work the same way. Think of a survey study as a 10,000-foot high view of the Bible. You probably won't pick up a lot of details from the survey itself, but once you have an idea of the overall layout of the map, it becomes much easier to go to a certain place on that map so you can see things close up and in greater detail.

For example, say you want to learn more about King David. Since you know he lived during the Old Covenant, you start with an Old Testament survey. From that study you learn that David lived during the ministry of the Prophet Samuel, so now you know you can go to the books of 1 Samuel and 2 Samuel to learn more.

For new Bible students, survey studies are something that they read in a survey study book. They don't create their own survey study, just like most people usually don't create their own maps. Instead, they find one that was created by an expert, and they follow that. There are many excellent Old and New Testament surveys that have been published, and if you are new to Bible study, they are a great place for you to get started.

You do have to keep in mind that these surveys of the Old and New Testaments are written by men, and sometimes their thoughts and opinions will seep into the content. The Bible is inspired by the Holy Spirit, but books written about the Bible are not. However, while this is always something you should keep in mind when reading books about the Bible, the general nature of survey studies makes it much less likely that false doctrines will be an issue.

In other words, because survey studies simply cover the broad outlines and structure of the Bible, you don't have to be as concerned about their authenticity as you do with other Bible study tools. You can find many good survey studie books online. Just be aware of any possible doctrinal biases or agendas on the part of the author.

This brings up another point: Part of developing a Bible student mindset is recognizing that you are going to have to begin building up your own Bible study library. That means over time you're going to be spending money to purchase books and buy new study tools. How much should you spend? Like the old joke goes, "How much have you got?" With very little effort, you could easily spend a small fortune on Bible study materials, but that isn't necessary when you're just getting started.

As we go through this book, I will identify what I consider to be the "absolutely essential" Bible study resources you should get, and the total cost of those materials will typically be less than $100. I will also show you many free resources, available online, that will often serve the same purpose as a book would. You do not have to go broke learning to study the Bible!

However, you should be willing to put some of your money toward Bible Study resources, because it's one of the few things you can invest in that could literally have an impact on your life for all of eternity. You also don't need to buy everything at once. You can add to your Bible study library a little bit at a time, and before long you'll have a substantial collection of resources which you can draw upon in your own studies.

As you become a more advanced Bible student, some interesting things will start to happen. Bible study resources that you used to rely on in your earlier days will become less meaningful to you. You might even find mistakes in those books, or discover that you disagree on some particular point with the expert who wrote the book. What many Bible students decide to do at that point is to start creating their own Bible Study resources.

If you're brand new to Bible study, I realize this is looking way ahead down the road for you, but I wanted to mention it anyway. It's not at all uncommon for advanced Bible students to create study materials based on their own studies, and to begin using those materials to teach others.

Just as reading a survey study is one of the first study methods a new Bible student will use, one of the first Bible study resources an advanced student will create on her own, is a survey study based on her own studying of the Bible.

Summary

The Bible is divided into 66 books, the 39 books of the Old Testament and the 27 books of the New Testament. Each Testament is further subdivided into five sections. The Old Testament is divided into the Pentateuch, the Historical Books, the Poetic Books, the Major Prophets, and the Minor prophets. The New Testament is divided into the Gospels, History (Acts), the Pauline Epistles, the General Epistles, and Prophecy (Revelation).

Understanding the layout of the Bible will help you in so many ways. It will make your Bible study time faster and more efficient. It will also help you to place the sermons you hear in their proper context, thus allowing you to get much more out of the messages you hear. Most importantly, knowing how the Bible is laid out will increase your confidence as you go forward in developing the mindset of a true student of the Bible.

While you may not think of a good study space as a "Bible study tool," the fact is that your Bible study efforts will be seriously hindered if you don't have a good study area set up for yourself. Many people think of Bible study as something lofty and spiritual, where God reveals His wisdom and hidden truths to us by His Spirit through the holy Scriptures. That is definitely one of the goals of Bible study.

Having a good study area may not seem as "spiritual," but by removing distractions you'll be able to focus in on the Word of God much more easily.

Finally, aside from your daily devotional reading, one of the best study methods that will help you to start getting acquainted with your Bible is the survey study. There are many excellent Old and New Testament surveys that have been published, and reading these survey books is a great place to get started with your own Bible study.

Eventually you'll need to start your own collection of Bible study books, and before long you'll have built that up into your personal Bible study library. There are also many survey studies available online. If you do a search for "Old Testament Survey" or "New Testament Survey" you'll be amazed at what you find. Just be careful to avoid doctrinal slants and men's opinions that are not entirely scriptural.

When you become a more advanced Bible student (note: even when you get to the "advanced" level, you'll still always be learning), you may have it on your heart to begin creating Bible study resources of your own. That can seem like a daunting task if you've never done it before, but the simple nature of the survey study makes it a great place to start.

So far we've covered how to get started with your Bible and how you can become more familiar with it. Now we're ready to zoom in from our 10,000-foot viewpoint, down to the microscopic level, where we will start investigating some of the hidden secrets of real Bible study, and then we'll slowly zoom out again from there.

Chapter 2 Discussion Questions

1. What does it mean to be a "God Approved" Bible student?

2. How will a consistent, daily devotion assist you as you explore other Bible study methods?

3. Why did God place more truth and revelation in the Bible than man can uncover in a lifetime?

4. The historical books continue the story of the nation of Israel. Why is their history relevant to the Christian church?

5. The Gospels of Matthew, Mark, Luke and John provide different accounts of the life and ministry of Jesus Christ. Why does the Bible offer four perspectives of Jesus' life?

6. How does the physical arrangement of your study space affect you? How does it affect your spiritual ability to receive revelation?

7. Do you get stressed when you hear the word "study"? What do you know about your own learning style? Do you remember better when you read it, hear it, or write it? How would knowing that help you study the Bible?

8. Why is it good to have a broad overview of the Bible?

9. Identify the total number of books in the Old and New Testaments, and in the Bible as a whole.

10. What are the categories of Bible books within the Old and New Testaments?

Chapter 3

Getting Around
The Word
Navigating the Bible

To whom will he teach knowledge,
and to whom will he explain the message?
Those who are weaned from the milk,
those taken from the breast?
For it is precept upon precept,
precept upon precept,
line upon line, line upon line,
here a little, there a little. – Isaiah 28:9, 10

The minister starts his sermon with, "Turn in your Bible to the Book of Hosea, chapter 4. Let us stand for the reading of God's Word" "Okay," you think to yourself as you stand up, "Hosea is one of the Minor Prophets, so that's in the Old Testament." You look down at your Bible and open it at the middle, finding yourself in the Book of Psalms. "Alright," you think, "Psalms is in the poetry section, and so if I go a little bit further toward the back, I'll hit the Major Prophets."

Turning past Proverbs you find the Book of Isaiah,

49

then you continue to flip past Jeremiah and Ezekiel. Coming to Daniel, you think, "Daniel is the last of the Major Prophets, so let me slow down. The books in the Minor Prophets are short and if I flip too far I'll wind up in the New Testament." Flipping slowly past Daniel you finally come to Hosea, but what did the preacher say? Hosea chapter 4! Moving past chapters 2 and 3, you come to chapter 4 and look up at the minister, waiting for him to tell you the verse where you should begin reading.

Many in the congregation are still frantically flipping through their Bibles, at least the ones who brought a Bible, trying to find Hosea. You notice others who have no Bible at all. They are standing passively, just waiting for the correct verse to be displayed on the screen. You whisper a silent prayer of thanksgiving to God, truly grateful that you've learned how to navigate your way through the Bible successfully.

This illustration is tragically repeated in church after church, week after week, all over the world. So many people don't know how to find specific passages within their own Bible, but you are learning better! You're becoming like the person above who was able to easily find Hosea chapter 4. The point isn't to fill your heart with pride because you know the Bible so well. The point is to help you recognize how truly empowering it can be to be able to locate specific Scriptures on your own.

Learning all about the layout of the Bible and making good use of survey studies will give you a good general overview of the Word of God, but learning to get around your Bible effectively is the key to finding specific verses and unlocking the spiritual treasures they contain.

Bible Reference Numbers

Each book of the Bible is divided into chapters, and those chapters are divided into verses. Specific Bible verses are notated by the name of the book, and then the chapter number and the verse number, separated by a colon. For example, the third chapter of John would be written as John 3. John 3:16 would be read as the Book of John, chapter 3, verse 16. If you read John 3:16-18, that would indicate the third chapter of John, verses 16 through 18.

The purpose of these Bible reference numbers is to help you find a particular passage of Scripture quickly and easily. Imagine if your Bible didn't have these reference numbers. Your Pastor might stand up on a Sunday morning and have to say something like, "Turn in your Bibles to the Book of Isaiah, go about 10 pages in, and then about halfway down the second column, assuming you have a Bible exactly like mine." How difficult would that be? No one would ever be able to find anything!

However, as helpful as these reference numbers are, it's important to remember that they weren't part of the original text. Think about letters you've written in the past. When I was dating my wife Katherine, her family went to Michigan to vacation for several weeks one summer. During that time, she wrote me several very sweet letters, and when I'd get one in the mail I would quickly open it to read her latest dispatch to me. Not one of those letters started out: "Chapter one. Verse one. Dearest Michael..."

Likewise, consider Paul's Epistle to the Ephesians. This was originally written as a letter from Paul to the church he started in the city of Ephesus. Have you ever written a letter to anyone before? Did you start with "Chapter One," and then divide the rest of your letter into chapters and verses? Neither did Paul! He simply sat down, and (inspired by the Holy Spirit) wrote a letter to his Christian brothers and sisters in that city.

The chapter and verse numbers were inserted much later. Stephen Langton was a professor in Paris working on editing a Latin version of the Bible in the year 1205. He introduced chapter divisions to make it easier for his readers to locate a specific passage. The Jews adopted his system for a new manuscript of the Hebrew Old Testament in 1330.

Then over 200 years later, in 1551, Robert Stephanus, who was a printer in Paris, inserted the verse divisions in the New Testament. Following Langton's chapter divisions, Stephanus divided the New Testament into verses while riding on horseback in the rain from Paris to Lyons, in order to meet a printer's deadline. The verse divisions in the Old Testament had been in place since about 200 A.D.

Since the chapter and verse numbers weren't a part of the original text, they should not be considered "inspired" in any way, shape, manner or form. Reference numbers are artificial additions to the organic writings of the Scriptures that were inserted centuries after the Bible was written. While they are helpful for the most part, they can also sometimes cause problems. Many times the chapter divisions will obscure an accurate reading of the text.

For example, the story of Nicodemus in John 3 actually begins at John 2:23 and continues into chapter 3.

Our habit is to read to the end of chapter 2, come to a "hard stop" there, and then later resume reading at the start of chapter 3. These artificial divisions might cause us to miss some of the natural continuity of the text. Therefore, chapter and verse numbers should always be thought of as a "finding guide," and never as a "reading guide."

Ignoring the chapter divisions while reading through a book of the Bible can be very illuminating, because you'll find connections between the chapters that you would otherwise miss if you let the chapter divisions dictate the boundaries of your Bible study. Try reading through a familiar book of the Bible, such as one of Paul's epistles, without paying attention to the chapter headings, and see if you notice anything new.

The same thing can happen with verse divisions, though not as often. Sometimes the men who inserted the verse divisions did so in odd places. In our English translations this is further compounded by the fact that there is no punctuation in ancient Hebrew. Because of this, occasionally you'll see a reference such as Genesis 2:4a, which indicates the Book of Genesis, chapter 2, verse 4, but only the first half of the verse.

One other thing to be aware of is that some books of the Bible are only one chapter long, such as Obadiah in the Old Testament, and Philemon, 2 John, 3 John, and Jude in the New Testament. Since these books are only one chapter, the chapter is omitted in the verse notation. For example, Philemon verse 6 would be written as Philemon 6, not Philemon 1:6. This can be confusing, since John 20 indicates John chapter 20, but Jude 20 is Jude verse 20.

Believe it or not, eventually you'll learn how many chapters are in each book of the Bible, so this will become less and less of a problem for you over time. Mastering the chapter and verse divisions in the books of the Bible will be a huge help to you over the course of your career as a Bible student. Also, when your Bible nerd friend tells you to turn to Acts 29 and you know there are only 28 chapters in Acts, you'll get the joke because by then you'll be a Bible nerd, too.

Bible Study Tools #3
Exhaustive Concordance

In chapter one we talked about finding a Bible you could use and get comfortable with, and last chapter we talked about setting up your study space. Now it's time to start looking at specific Bible study tools, starting with an exhaustive concordance. In my opinion, aside from the Bible itself, this is the single most important study tool that a new Bible student can have. If you don't have one yet, put it at the top of your list.

What is a concordance? A concordance is a reference book that lists all the words that are contained in the Bible. If you know part of a Bible verse, it's a great tool for finding out where that verse is located. It's also extremely useful for starting a word study, which is the study of a specific word in the Bible, what it means, and how it is used.

The term "exhaustive" means that it contains every single word that's included in the Bible, leaving none of them out. Some concordances include only the most common words that people want to look up, and they highlight only certain verses in which those words appear. They don't contain every word and every verse. However, for study purposes you will definitely want an exhaustive concordance.

(Disclaimer: Throughout this book I will make Bible study tool recommendations to you based on my experience and best judgment. I receive no compensation for any of these and would not accept any if offered. This allows me to make authentic recommendations that you can trust.)

The two most popular exhaustive concordances on the market today are *Strong's Exhaustive Concordance* and *Young's Analytical Concordance,* both of which have published editions that match the main Bible versions that are available. Both are excellent, but I recommend Strong's over Young's for two reasons: First, Strong's is more popular, so it's in wider use. Second, because it is in wider use, the Strong's reference numbers are used in many other Bible study publications. I will explain what is meant by the term "Strong's reference numbers" shortly.

Strong's Concordance is divided into 4 main sections:

1)   Main Concordance
2)   Appendix
3)   Dictionary of Hebrew Words
4)   Dictionary of Greek Words

The rest of this section will break down the layout of Strong's Concordance. If you already own a copy, it would be helpful for you to have it handy so you can follow along in your copy of Strong's Concordance as you read.

The Main Concordance

This section lists alphabetically every word that appears in the Bible. It is the largest section, taking up about 90% of the concordance. At the top of each page are guide words for easier navigation, similar to the pages of a dictionary.

The word entries are listed in columns. Each line entry for a given word appears underneath in its Biblical order, from the Old Testament to the New Testament. For example, let's say we wanted to look at how the word "peace" was used in the Gospel of John. First we'd look up the word peace, and then we'd go down the column through the Old Testament entries, past the first three Gospels, and finally we'd find some entries in the Book of John that looked like this:

14:27	**P** I leave with you, my peace I give unto you	G1515
14:27	Peace I leave with you, my **p** I give unto you	G1515
16:33	in me ye might have **p**. In the world ye	G1515
20:19	and saith unto them, **P** be unto you	G1515
20:21	Then said Jesus to them again, **P** be	G1515
20:26	in the midst, and said, **P** be unto you.	G1515

The first thing on each line is the chapter and verse listing. Next is a short excerpt from that verse, giving some of the words that appear before and after the word we're looking up. To save space, the actual word itself is written only as a single bolded letter. In newer versions, the words of Christ are highlighted (similar to having the words of Christ in red in the Bible). Finally, at the end of the line entry is the Strong's Reference number for that word.

Strong's Reference Numbers

The Old Testament was originally written in Hebrew, and the New Testament was originally written in Greek. The Bibles we read today are translations from those original languages. That means an English word we read in a given verse has been translated from either a Hebrew word, if found in the Old Testament, or a Greek word, if found in the New Testament.

Sometimes more than one Greek or Hebrew word will be translated using the same English word. There isn't a one-to-one correlation between them. Also, the Hebrew and Greek words in the Bible can be translated into several different English words. It can start to get a little confusing, but that's where the Strong's reference numbers come in, to help us keep everything sorted out.

In the example above from John, we see that the word translated "peace" in all six verses is Strong's reference number G1515. The G is short for Greek, indicating this word can be found in the concordance's Greek dictionary. Likewise, Old Testament Strong's reference numbers start with "H" for Hebrew.

Words with no Strong's reference numbers indicate a word that doesn't appear in the original text, but was simply added by the translators to add clarity to the meaning of the verse. In most Bible versions, these words appear in italics to indicate that they were not part of the original Greek or Hebrew text. Malachi 3:10 is a good example.

Now that we have the Strong's reference number for

the word "peace" in John – G1515 – we're ready to look it up in the Greek dictionary so we can learn more about it.

Strong's Greek and Hebrew Dictionaries

The main concordance is the largest part of Strong's Exhaustive Concordance. Following that is the Appendix, which contains a full listing of all the minor words in the Bible (articles, conjunctions, and prepositions, such as "the," "and," and "in"). At the back of Strong's Concordance you will find the Hebrew and Greek dictionaries.

These dictionaries contain every Hebrew and Greek word found in the Bible. The words are listed with their associated Strong's reference number, according to their order in the Hebrew or Greek alphabets. Once again, remember that Strong's reference numbers are useful because they are used literally everywhere in Bible reference materials. You will run into them over and over again in your career as a Bible student.

Dictionary entries are similar to the line entries in the main concordance. They begin with the Strong's reference number. Next comes the lexical form of the word, which is the original word in either Hebrew or Greek type, followed by an English transliteration of the word.

If there are any related Hebrew or Greek words, they are given by Strong's number. Next comes a basic definition of the word. Finally, the English translation is listed following a colon and a dash ":-"

Here's an example from our Greek word *eirene:*

"**G1515   eirene** probably from a primary verb *eiro* (to join); *peace* (literal or figurative); by implication, *prosperity*: - one, peace, quietness, rest, set at one again"

In the example above, we see the original Greek word is *eirene,* and that it is related to the Greek verb that means "to join" (which already begins to give us some insight as to what Bible peace is really all about). Next comes the definition, where we learn the word can refer to literal or figurative peace, and it can also imply prosperity. Finally, after the colon and the dash, we see that *eirene* is translated into all of these words in the English Bible: *one, peace, quietness, rest,* and *set at one again.*

It should be noted that the Greek and Hebrew dictionaries found in Strong's Concordance are very basic. To fully understand the way a Greek or Hebrew word is used in the Bible, it's necessary to learn the languages. However, with the understanding that possessing a concordance doesn't automatically make you a Greek and Hebrew scholar, you will find that learning to use Strong's Concordance, in association with your other Bible study activities, can be extremely empowering.

Using Your Strong's Concordance

There are many uses for your concordance and these will be covered throughout the rest of this book. One of the most traditional uses is finding a particular Bible reference when you remember only part of the verse. For example, if I wanted to find where Jesus said the words, *"Peace I leave with you,"* I might look up the word "peace" or the word "leave," and then go down the column through all the entries until I found the verse I was looking for, which in this case would be John 14:27.

When using your concordance for a verse search, start with the least common words you can remember from the verse, because it usually makes the process easier. For instance, if I didn't know where John 3:16 was in the Bible but I remembered the phrase, "For God so loved the world that He gave..." then I probably wouldn't look up the word "God" to try to find that verse, since that word is used thousands of times in the Bible. Instead, I'd look up "loved" or "world" first to try to find the Bible reference. When you find the Bible reference you are looking for, make sure that you take a moment to look it up in your Bible in order to confirm that it's the right one.

Of course, today anyone can type part of a Bible verse they remember into a search engine on their phone or computer and easily find the Bible reference, which means that concordances are no longer the most common way to look up a verse number. However, the other advantages of an exhaustive concordance still remain. It's still the best place to look at all the uses of a given Bible word listed together in one place, and it is the foundational tool for several different Bible study methods.

Furthermore, while computerized concordances found within the top Bible software programs are usually good, many of the free concordances available online contain errors. With so many entries it's easy for a web designer to make a mistake, and I've even found similar errors in the various Bible software titles, though not so many. Therefore, I strongly recommend that you double check any electronic concordance listing with the hard copy to insure your study is as accurate as possible.

Bible Study Method #3
Word Studies

The other major use of an exhaustive concordance is a Bible study method called a word study. While the survey study gives you a great bird's-eye view, the word study zooms all the way in to literally focus on a single word. Not only is it very exciting to uncover new Bible truths by using a word study, but this Bible study method is the foundation for all of the other study methods that will follow.

A common misconception of word studies is that they are studies of words that appear in the English version of the Bible. A word study is not a study of the English word, but rather it's a study of that word in the original language. Put differently, a word study is actually the study of how a particular Hebrew or Greek word is used in the Bible.

Your Bible studies will typically be divided into what I call quick studies and in-depth studies. A quick study is when you just need to look something up or get a quick question answered. An in-depth study takes longer, covers a deeper and broader range of material, and can even branch out into additional related studies. Both types often begin with a basic word study.

Here are the steps to a profitable word study:

Step 1 – Decide what word you want to study

This part is pretty easy. Maybe you heard a preacher say something in a message that piqued your curiosity and you want to follow up, or perhaps you have a question about what a certain verse means. When you're hungry for the things of God, it's not hard to come up with a whole list of things you'd like to learn more about. The most challenging aspect of this step is narrowing your word list down to just one single word.

Step 2 – See how often the word is used in Scripture

Look up the word in your concordance and see if it's a word that's used hundreds of times or just a few times. If it's a word that's used a lot in the Bible, you may be looking at a more in-depth study. On the other hand, the frequency with which a word is used can also give insights. For example, a word study on the word "faith" would probably be more worthwhile than one on the word "dragons."

As one preacher put it, "We should major on the majors, and minor on the minors." In other words, we should be spending the majority of our study time on things the Bible emphasizes, and less time on things the Bible mentions less frequently.

Step 3 – Identify the Strong's number for that word

This step is also easy. Look up the word in Strong's

and find the reference number. For example, if I wanted to study the word "faith" in the New Testament, I would find that the Strong's number is G4102.

Step 4 – Look up the Greek or Hebrew word

Next, look the word up in the Hebrew or Greek dictionary, whichever applies. Following our example, I would find that G4102 is the Greek word *pistis*, along with the definition. I would also discover that *pistis* is translated into the English words "assurance, belief, believe, faith, and fidelity."

Step 5 – Use other research tools to gain further insights

Once again, the Greek and Hebrew dictionaries found at the back of Strong's Concordance are very basic. In order to gain a more complete understanding of the word, it may be useful to consult other research tools, such as *Vine's Expository Dictionary of New Testament Words* or a lexical study Bible, both of which will be fully described in later chapters.

Following Up

At this point I have a decision to make. If I am just looking for a quick definition, then I'm done. However, if I want to do an in-depth study on the subject of faith, there are many, many verses containing the word *pistis*, which indicates to me that this particular study will take a significant amount of time. In-depth word studies are actually the first building block of many other Bible study methods, which is why we are covering them first before moving on to those other methods.

Summary

Understanding Bible reference numbers is the key to being able to find your way through your Bible effectively. Knowing whether a given verse is located in the Old or New Testament, and which section of books it's a part of will be very helpful to you. Knowing the location of a particular Bible passage can give you context that can increase your general understanding of the verse.

At the same time, it's important that we don't get hung up by chapter and verse numbers. The Bible was originally written by people who were inspired by the Holy Spirit, but otherwise they were just like you and me. Letters should be read as letters, poetry as poetry, history as history, etc.

Once you know the basics of navigating your Bible, you'll be able to make use of tools such as an exhaustive concordance. Aside from your Bible, Strong's Concordance is probably the most important Bible study tool you can own, and it's one that you will come back to again and again.

Strong's Concordance can be used to look up verses, and also to find out which Hebrew and Greek words were used in translating our English Bible. It's also a very effective tool for performing word studies.

The word study is a Bible study method that focuses on a single word in the Bible and explores how it is used. The goal of a word study is to gain a deeper understanding of what the word means. Word studies can be quick studies to look up a definition or answer simple questions. They are also the foundational building blocks of more in-depth Bible study methods.

In chapter one we talked about devotional Bible reading, which should already be a part of your daily routine, right? Chapter two encouraged you to begin developing a Bible student mentality, and to begin seeing yourself from this point forward as a lifelong student of God's Word.

In both chapters two and three we also covered a lot of technical, yet very practical, things needed to get you even more prepared for successful Bible study. You also got a glimpse of the exciting possibilities for spiritual growth that good Bible studying can open up to you, through survey studies and word studies.

In a way, it's been somewhat like packing for a trip you've been anticipating for a long time. You're excited to be going on the trip, and you understand why taking the time to properly pack is important, but now you're ready to get going! I truly understand how you feel. Just remember that preparation time is never wasted time. The more you follow through on the action steps covered in the first three chapters, the better positioned you'll be for real Bible study success. My purpose for making sure you get everything packed up correctly ahead of time is to insure that you'll get the maximum benefit from your trip.

Chapter 3 Discussion Questions

1. Given today's technology, is it still necessary for Christians to know how to navigate their Bibles? If so, why?

2. How will knowing how to navigate your Bible help you share Christ with others?

3. Have you ever seen a John 3:16 sign at a football game? Does it mean anything to someone who is a Bible illiterate? Why or why not?

4. What is a concordance? How does an "exhaustive" concordance differ from a general concordance?

5. What are the 4 main sections of Strong's Concordance?

6. You learn a co-worker's mom has just died. You want to encourage her with a few Bible verses. Using your concordance, how might you locate some appropriate verses?

7. The italicized words which appear in some Bibles were not included in the original text. Why were these words added by the translators? (see Malachi 3:10 for example)

8. How can knowing the meaning of a word in the original text (Hebrew or Greek) increase your understanding of a Bible verse?

9. Is it possible to be led by the Spirit through Bible study books? Can you make a spiritual connection with God while reading a book about the Bible? How would that be different from being led by the Holy Spirit at church?

Chapter 4

I Heard An Old, Old Story

Understanding the Theme of the Bible

So Philip ran to him and heard him reading Isaiah the prophet and asked, "Do you understand what you are reading?" – Acts 8:30

The first three chapters of this book cover what I call "Bible mechanics," which means the basic knowledge and tools that are necessary for a new Bible student to get started. If you don't have a basic understanding of the layout of the Bible, or if you don't know how to look up a Bible verse yet, then you really need to get that down before you can move on to anything more advanced.

Survey studies are a great way to increase your familiarity with the Bible, and word studies are an excellent way to put Bible verses under the microscope to find the inspiring revelations they contain. However, survey studies give you only a very basic framework of the Bible, and word studies on their own are limited as well.

Consider the word "run." What does "run" mean? The answer to that question is: "It depends." If we're looking at "run" as a noun it can mean a lot of things. It can mean a path joggers follow, a score in a baseball game, a printing of a book, or a small stream, among many other things. If we also look at "run" as a verb then literally dozens more meanings are added to the list of possibilities. So how can we know which "run" is meant?

This illustrates the weakness of isolated word studies. Just as English words often have many possible meanings, so do Greek and Hebrew words. To interpret the meaning of a given word accurately, we need to examine it in the context in which it is used. To make things even more challenging, there are many different contexts that can have an impact on a word's meaning, such as its literary, historical, or cultural contexts, to name just a few.

The next key to successful Bible study that we're going to begin looking at is not just meaning, but meaning within context. We're going to start with context within the overall story. The first context to identify, when examining a particular Bible passage, is where does it fall within the context of the overall story of the Bible?

The Story of the Bible

The Bible is God's holy, inspired Word. It's Heaven's instruction manual for our lives and our guidebook for wise and holy living. It's a masterpiece of literature and history unequaled anywhere in the world. It's the best-selling book of all time, and it's the foundation of all Christian faith and practice.

However, the real reason the Bible has endured over the centuries is that it is a truly amazing story. In fact, as stories go, the Bible has it all. This season's latest TV series can't touch the drama and suspense contained in the Bible. Seriously.

As a Bible student, there are a couple of good reasons you need to learn the story of the Bible. For one thing, as already mentioned, it will help you put individual passages in their proper context. Another thing you'll find when you start learning the Bible's story is that it makes studying the Bible a lot more interesting, and a big factor in being able to learn and understand a subject is whether or not you're interested in it.

When the dry technicalities of the Hebrew and Greek are fleshed out with the emotional pull of the Bible's story, your interest level will naturally increase, motivating you to dig in even more. This increased desire to study, motivated by intense interest, can at times be of greater benefit than knowing the correct context of a passage.

So what is the story of the Bible? Each of the 66 books in the Bible tells its own story, but together they become part of an over-arching tale that covers literally thousands of years. Think of it like one of those television series where there's a story arc that's spread over several seasons. Within each season there are episodes, and each of those episodes usually contains an A and a B storyline. Yet, they all come together as parts of the arc that is the overall story.

In the Bible, the stories within each book are like the episodes in the example above. The books of the Bible could correspond to TV seasons, and the entire Bible as a whole contains the story arc of the entire series. Many of the stories in the Bible are considered amazing episodes in their own right, valued for their content by Christians and non-Christians alike, such as the story of David and Goliath or the story of the Prodigal Son.

Yet these are just swipes of cloth that come together with many others to form the rich tapestry of the Bible's overall story. So what is the story of the Bible? What makes it so interesting? I'm going to give the highlights here, with the goal of illustrating the overall story arc for you, but the reality is you're going to spend the rest of your life as a Bible student learning and enjoying the details of this story.

Our story begins, literally, at the beginning. The opening chapters of Genesis cover Creation, the Fall, and the terrible results of the Fall. Here the stage is set for all that will follow. God creates Adam and Eve in their garden paradise and gives them dominion over the entire Earth under His authority. Satan enters in and tricks Adam and Eve into surrendering their authority to him, and now instead of Adam and Eve being in dominion under God, Satan has dominion over them and all of their descendants.

Even as God evicts them out of Eden, He prophesies how all of this will end: A descendant of the woman will come, and while Satan will be able to hurt him at first, this Savior will ultimately crush Satan's head (the head symbolizing authority). The remainder of the Bible, from Genesis 3:24 until the Book of Revelation, is about God working to fulfill this prophecy, and to rescue His planet and the people He created from Satan's captivity. That is the overall story arc.

The first 11 chapters of Genesis cover at least 1600 years of history, until a man named Abraham comes along. Finally, God has a man He can work with, and so He makes a covenant with Him, the benefits of which will be passed down through Abraham's descendants. Abraham has a son named Isaac, who has a son named Jacob, and Jacob has twelve sons whose descendants become the twelve tribes of the nation of Israel.

God sends prophets to Israel to speak for Him, and while wars and political intrigue continue among the nations, there is a parallel unseen war raging in the spirit realm, where the demons of the kingdom of darkness are struggling mightily to prevent God's words in Eden from coming to pass. The prophecies of the prophets also continue laying the groundwork for the descendant of Eve, who finally comes as a baby named Jesus, born of God to a young virgin named Mary.

Jesus grows up. Outwardly He appears to be a failed leader due to His criminal trial and crucifixion. However, in reality He fights a spiritual battle in which He dies, goes to Hell, and takes back Adam's authority from Satan, culminating in His victorious resurrection from the dead. From that point until today, the people of Earth have been set free forever from the dominion of Satan. They just need someone to tell them.

Now that is an interesting story! And knowing that story arc, you can now start placing the individual "episodes" you read in the Bible within the Bible's overall theme, which is the redemption of mankind from the bondage of sin through the power and ministry of Jesus Christ. Obviously I could have gone into much greater detail, but why take the thrill of discovery away from you? Learn to look for clues that fit into this story-arc as you study the Bible.

One good example is Acts chapter 7, where Stephen is about to be stoned to death by the Pharisees for preaching about Christ, but not before they go through the formality of a show trial. When Stephen gets his chance to testify, he launches into a speech describing the Bible's story arc from Abraham all the way to his present day. The result is a thumbnail sketch of almost the entire Old Testament, a great benefit for the Bible student!

As you read through the Bible, be on the lookout for places where pieces of the story arc get filled in. In the example of the television series we discussed earlier, there are always certain episodes in a story-arc type of series where key parts of the storyline are shown to the viewer in a "big reveal." Look for these types of themed "episodes" among the stories that make up the story-arc of the Bible.

Bible Study Tools #4
Parallel Bibles & Study Bibles

Once you have a Bible for everyday reading, along with a copy of Strong's Exhaustive Concordance, the next Bible study tools you should look into are Parallel Bibles and Study Bibles. These two kinds of Bibles will really open up a lot of new study possibilities, and both are very useful in the Bible study method we're going to learn about next.

Parallel Bibles

As you are probably already aware, there are many different Bible versions available. We're going to look at how to go about choosing a Bible version in chapters 8, 9 and 10, including the advantages and disadvantages of the King James Version (KJV), but one key advantage of looking at a Scripture passage in multiple Bible versions is that you can gain deeper insights by comparing them to one another.

However, it can quickly become very difficult to keep three or four different Bible versions spread out so you can perform these kinds of side by side comparisons. That's where a parallel Bible comes in very handy. Parallel Bibles contain multiple Bible translations side by side, so you can easily look at a verse in different Bible versions. Often you will find that other translations will reveal more light within a particular verse.

It will become a normal thing for you to consult multiple translations during Bible study in addition to the KJV and your preferred version. A parallel Bible makes it very easy to compare different translations quickly. Two of the best parallel Bibles available are *The Comparative Study Bible* and *The Word From 26 Translations*.

Study Bibles

Study Bibles are Bibles with additional study notes added to the margins of each page. They may also have additional sections of notes in the back. Study Bibles can be very helpful with defining archaic words, explaining strange cultural customs, examining textual variances, and helping with the study of major Bible topics. Examples include the *Scofield Reference Bible, Dake's Annotated Bible,* the *Life Application Study Bible,* and the *Thompson Chain Reference Bible.*

However, despite their incredible benefits, there are also some problems regarding the use of study Bibles, and we need to be aware of these potential dangers so our Bible study efforts aren't spent going in the wrong direction.

The first danger of study Bibles that we must be aware of is the frailty of human interpretation. The words of the Bible on each page are inspired by God and we can rely on them, putting our faith and trust in God's Word completely. However, the study notes on the same page are not divinely inspired. They are the work of a fallible man, and while the author of the study notes is most likely a highly qualified Bible scholar, there is still the possibility that he could be incorrect.

For example, both the *Scofield* and *Dake's Study Bibles* contain study notes promoting the so-called "gap theory." The gap theory alleges that potentially millions of years of time passed between Genesis 1:1 and Genesis 1:2, an idea that many accept, while many others don't believe it is supported by the biblical text, myself included. However, if you were a new Bible student and you saw this information in the study notes in the margin of your Bible, you might accept it without question.

Whether the gap theory is true or not is irrelevant to

my point. It's just an illustration. The point is that when using a study Bible it can be very easy to transpose the authority of the Scripture text to the words of the study notes if you're not careful. Always remember that while the Bible is divinely inspired, the study notes are simply the opinion of one man, probably a very knowledgeable man, but still just a man. Whenever you use a study Bible, always make sure you're separating the study notes from the text of the Scriptures.

Doctrinal slants are the second danger to beware of with study Bibles. In this case however, rather than dealing with the opinion of the scholar who wrote the study notes, you're dealing with the denominational beliefs behind it. That's why it's always a good idea to find out the theological background of the person who wrote the study notes.

For example, the *Thompson Chain Reference Bible* was developed in 1890 by Frank C. Thompson, who was a good Methodist. This is an absolutely excellent study Bible, containing thousands of links within its superb chain-reference system. However, if your goal is to learn more about the baptism in the Holy Spirit and speaking in other tongues, this work will be of little use to you because Dr. Thompson didn't believe in that.

The final danger to beware of when using a study Bible is the limitations of human memory. Even people who have good memories find that clarity can get muddied with the passage of time. When using a study Bible extensively, it can be easy to accidentally confuse something you read in the notes with something you read in the Bible text.

Always take into consideration the possibility that you might be remembering something incorrectly, and double check it against the source before you accidentally share incorrect information with others. Now, while sharing these few potential pitfalls of study Bibles, I sincerely hope I haven't scared you away from them.

Study Bibles are an excellent source of knowledge and insight, and they can save you an incredible amount of time. I definitely recommend adding a good study Bible to your collection of Bible study tools, and if you're forced to choose between them, I would suggest purchasing a good study Bible over a parallel Bible. Of course, over the course of time you'll probably wind up owning both anyway.

Cross Referencing

Many Bibles that are not true "study" Bibles will still contain a center cross-reference, which is a column of Bible references going down the middle of the page, between the two columns of Bible text. For example, you might be reading a verse and notice a small letter "a" above the verse. Looking over to the center reference column, you'll find the same letter "a" with one or more other Scriptures listed beside it.

These will be Scripture verses that are somehow related to the verse you started on, and flipping over to read them will likely give you more understanding of the starting Scripture. Sometimes it's fun to just keep following the cross references to see where they lead. The *Thompson Chain Reference Bible,* in addition to being a very good study Bible, uses cross-referencing on steroids!

Cross-referencing makes it easy to follow threads of thought throughout Scripture, without having to consult an additional outside reference work. If you can't get a true study Bible yet, do try to get a devotional Bible with cross-references for your everyday use.

Bible Study Method #4
Verse Studies

As you have probably realized by now, the Bible study tools introduced in each chapter usually correspond with the Bible study methods introduced in the same chapter. Previously we looked at word studies, which is the study of the meaning of individual words in the Bible. Now we're going to look at verse studies.

A verse study is performed to enable you to understand the meaning of a particular verse or verses, and to answer the questions, "What does this verse mean? What does it teach me?" Here are the steps to a Bible verse study:

Step 1 – Identify the source of the verse

Imagine reading a magazine containing both news stories and poems. You would read the poetry differently than you would the prose of the news story because they are two different kinds of literature. Be aware of the book and book division of the Bible where the Scripture passage is found. This will help you interpret which type of literature the verse is and how it should be read.

Step 2 – Read the entire chapter

Read the entire chapter where the Scripture passage appears. Take special note of the verses before and after your specific verse. This will help you see the correct context of the verse.

Step 3 – Pray about the verse

Ask the Lord to teach you by His Spirit, "What does this verse teach? What is the practical application of it for me today?" Do this before looking at any outside study materials, because those might give you preconceived ideas which could cause you to miss the voice of the Spirit.

Step 4 – Research the verse

To help you better understand the verse, use Bible study tools such as Bible dictionaries, a concordance, commentaries, and Hebrew/Greek word studies. I'm sure it's already clear to you how a parallel Bible or a good study Bible can be of great benefit in helping you understand the meaning of a verse.

Step 5 – Analyze the verse

This is the key step. All of the other steps lead up to this one: Read through the verse and write down notes about anything you see within the verse.

Now read it a second time. Every time you see something new that the verse teaches, write it down. "This verse teaches _____." Repeat this process at least 10 times, reading the verse and writing down what it teaches. Double that would be better, but when you're getting started, it's hard to see as much as you'll be able to after you've been doing it for a while.

> **For the word of God is living and active, sharper than any two-edged sword, piercing to the division of soul and of spirit, of joints and of marrow, and discerning the thoughts and intentions of the heart. - Hebrews 4:12**

The Word of God is literally inexhaustible. There will always be new nuggets of insight you can mine from a verse, no matter how many times you've looked at it before. It will amaze you how much you'll find in a single verse, in just one sitting, each time you go through it again for this exercise.

Following Up

As with all Bible study tools and methods, there are some things you'll want to watch out for. First, never include anything in your analysis that doesn't appear directly within the verse. Make a real effort to keep your own tradition and bias out of your analysis.

Also, don't give up too soon! Make sure you find everything you can in that verse. Keep digging until it seems like there's absolutely nothing left for you to find. Then take all the information you've gathered from all the analysis runs and combine them into a list or paragraph, whatever works for you. The result of these efforts should prove to you that you now have a much greater understanding of that verse.

File the page away in your study notes so you can refer to it later. Even though you think you've pulled everything from the verse that you possibly can, odds are that after some time has passed, if you look at it again, you'll find new things in that verse that you missed the first time. This is a natural result that happens when you continue to grow spiritually through the Word and prayer.

Summary

While the definitions of Bible words are important, their context is usually much more important because the context can have a bearing on a word's actual meaning. The first place a new Bible student can find meaning through context is within the context of the Bible's story.

The Bible contains a story-arc that tracks through all 66 books, from beginning to end. That story-arc is a cosmic tale describing God's efforts to win back his creation and the people through the work of Jesus Christ. Understanding the story of the Bible will help you put specific passages within their correct context, and also motivate you toward further study by increasing your interest in the Bible as you look for new clues and you seek to fit them into the overall story-arc.

Parallel Bibles are an excellent way to gain deeper insights into the meaning of a Bible verse, and study Bibles contain additional study notes in the margins that can also add clarity. Study Bibles are an incredibly helpful resource, but we must remember that the study notes were written by men, and they are not inspired in the same way as the actual Bible text. In addition to parallel and study Bibles, a Bible with a good cross-reference can be extremely helpful as you strive to determine the meaning of a Bible verse.

Verse studies are the next step up from word studies. The result of a good verse study will answer the questions, "What does this verse mean?" and "What is it teaching me?" By analyzing the Bible verse following the verse study method, you will be able to gain a stunning amount of insight into the revelation which that verse contains.

Picture yourself as a miner trying to find gems, precious stones, and nuggets of gold to dig out of the earth. Instead of a map and a pickaxe you have survey studies, concordances, and study Bibles. Most miners can dig out only physical nuggets of gold, but you are being trained and empowered to dig out nuggets of truth which are eternal.

Chapter 4 Discussion Questions

1. What is meant by the term "story arc" of the Bible, and why is understanding it vital to the Bible student?

2. How does knowing the structure of the Bible help you to better understand the Bible? How does knowing the purpose of the text add to the meaning?

3. How does the expression "missing the forest for all of the trees" relate to the books of the Bible and the story arc of the Bible?

4. How do the life stories of Moses, David, or Elijah contribute to the Bible's overall story arc, which is the redemption of mankind by God?

5. Compare and contrast Parallel Bibles versus Study Bibles. In what situations would each one be helpful?

6. What is the advantage of looking at a Scripture through multiple Bible versions using a Parallel Bible?

7. What are some pitfalls to be aware of when using a Study Bible?

8. How can using a center cross-reference be helpful?

9. What are the key questions you want to answer in a Verse Study? How does a Verse Study help you find those answers?

Chapter 5

Decently And In Order
The Original Layout of the Bible

*But all things should be done decently
and in order. - 1 Corinthians 14:40*

Once you have an idea of the story of the Bible, it doesn't take long to discover that the books of the Bible don't really follow the order of its story. This can be frustrating for the new Bible student who's just starting out. Reading the Bible can sometimes feel like watching a Quentin Tarantino movie: The story is great, but why is it out of order? It's like seeing the opening act of a play, followed by the third and fourth acts and then the second and fifth acts.

There's a reason the Bible, as we have it today, seems out of order. *It's because the Bible we have today is out of order.* It may surprise you to learn that none of the Bibles on the market today follow the arrangement of books as laid out in the original manuscripts. That may sound crazy to you, but it's true nonetheless. There's not necessarily an evil conspiracy behind it all. It just happens to be the way our Bibles are today.

For various reasons that will be explained going

forward, Bible publishers have avoided producing a Bible that places the books in their correct manuscript order. This has resulted in the vast number of translations available today which contain the mixed up arrangement. What's even more interesting is that when the books of the Bible are placed in their original order, they actually follow the Bible's story-arc with a consistency that will amaze you.

The Original Layout of the Bible

As a Bible student you should know the original layout of the Bible, not only to be informed, but also because knowing the Bible's original manuscript form will make it easier for you to understand it.

The Original Old Testament

The original order of the Hebrew manuscript of the Old Testament is as follows:

I. The Law (Torah)
1. Genesis
2. Exodus
3. Leviticus
4. Numbers
5. Deuteronomy

II. The Prophets
6. Joshua and Judges *(considered as one book by the Judeans before the 2nd century)*
7. Book of Kingdoms *(Samuel and Kings – also considered as one book by the Judeans)*

8. Isaiah
9. Jeremiah
10. Ezekiel
11. The Book of the Twelve *(Hosea to Malachi – always considered as one book by the Judeans)*

II. The Writings *(which is also sometimes called "The Psalms" after the first book in this collection)*

12. Psalms
13. Proverbs
14. Job
15. Song of Solomon
16. Ruth
17. Lamentations
18. Ecclesiastes
19. Esther
20. Daniel
21. Ezra-Nehemiah *(considered as one book by the Judeans)*
22. Chronicles *(considered as one book by the Judeans)*

This arrangement of the Old Testament, into 22 books, represents exactly the same material that is contained within the 39 books in our Bibles today, they are just ordered and numbered differently. In the original numeration, the number of books agreed with the number of letters in the Hebrew alphabet.

The Law, or Torah, was for Israel a document similar to what the Constitution of the United States is for us today. It codified the laws of the nation which God gave to Moses, and was read aloud to the entire nation once every year (Deuteronomy 31:9-13). The Torah was placed in the center of the Temple, within the Holy of Holies, because it represented God's supreme position of power and authority, making it the foundation upon which the remaining 17 books of the Old Testament stood.

Next come the Prophets. Throughout the Bible the Prophets are portrayed as having greater rank than Kings, such as when the prophet Nathan commanded King David (2 Samuel 12), or when the prophets Elijah and Elisha instructed the kings of Israel and the surrounding nations.

Even the prophet Jonah was sent to the ruler of Assyria to tell him what God wanted him to do. This is the reason the Prophets Division follows the books of the Law of Moses. They were next in line in the order of divine authority.

The Prophets Division can be further subdivided into three parts, and this subdivision is based on the biblical principle of eldership. Eldership meant honoring the older leaders in the community with a higher social rank. This principle can be observed throughout the Bible, from the elders of Israel (Exodus 3:16) all the way to the 24 elders surrounding the throne of God in Heaven (Revelation 4:4).

There were also degrees of rank among the Old Testament prophets based on eldership, which can be seen in the way the prophetic books in the original Old Testament were arranged. Those three sections are:

1) The Former Prophets
　　　(Joshua-Judges and the Book of Kingdoms)

2) The Latter Prophets
  (Isaiah, Jeremiah, and Ezekiel)
3) The Minor Prophets
  (the 12 books from Hosea to Malachi).

As you can easily see, in the original Old Testament the books that were written first come before those which were written later. This chronological arrangement of the Former Prophets following the principle of eldership makes much more sense than the order of biblical books we have today. We will examine this further in the next chapter when we take a look at how all these different books were gathered into the Bible we have today.

The third division of the Old Testament, as it was arranged in the original manuscripts, was called the Psalms or the Writings. The books in the Writings are not placed in chronological order as with the first two divisions of the original Old Testament.

Instead, these eleven books are all related to the Kings of Israel or have a royal theme, so they are next in line after The Prophets. Even the Lord Jesus Christ recognized this arrangement of the Bible during His ministry on Earth:

Then he said to them, "These are my words that I spoke to you while I was still with you, that everything written about me in the <u>Law of Moses</u> and <u>the Prophets</u> and <u>the Psalms</u> must be fulfilled." Then he opened their minds to understand the Scriptures. - Luke 24:44-45

Here Jesus calls the third division of books "the Psalms," but He was actually referring to the complete third division, not just the Book of Psalms by itself. In the first century this section had no technical name, so it was sometimes called "the Other Books" or the "Writings."

Later it became common practice to identify this section as "The Psalms," because that was the name of the largest book in the group, and also the book with which the third division of the Old Testament began.

The Latin Vulgate

Jerome was a Christian teacher and theologian in the late 4th century, and he wanted a Bible translated into his own Latin tongue. All of the Bible translations available in his day were written in Greek, but there were parts of the Roman Empire where only Latin was spoken.

These Greek Bible translations were based on the Hebrew Septuagint (pronounced *sep-TU-a-jint*), which was a translation of the Old Testament Scriptures into Greek. This translation was created for Greek-speaking Jews who didn't speak Hebrew. It was called the Septuagint because it was created by 70 Jewish scholars in Alexandria, Egypt.

The Septuagint also contained books which the Jews did not regard as Holy Scripture, but were included anyway for their historical and cultural value. Jerome realized these books weren't part of the Bible, but he was compelled by the church to include them also. These became the books that we know today as the Apocrypha, the additional Old Testament books included in Roman Catholic Bibles.

Jerome thought these books were useful to be read by the church for encouragement. However, they were not to be recognized as canonical books, meaning they weren't to be considered as official books of the Bible, or books used to establish Christian doctrine.

The Latin Vulgate Bible took 20 years to produce, and was completed in 405 AD. For reasons we will examine later in this chapter, Jerome changed the order of the New Testament books in his Bible, and the original layout of the 22 Old Testament books was also abandoned in his Bible.

However, prior to the completion of the Latin Vulgate, even Jerome acknowledged this original arrangement of the Old Testament into twenty-two books:

"As, then, there are twenty-two elementary characters by means of which we write in Hebrew all we say, and the compass of the human voice is contained within their limits, so we reckon twenty-two books, by which, as by the alphabet of the doctrine of God, a righteous man is instructed in tender infancy, and, as it were, while still at the breast." - Jerome, Preface to Samuel and Kings

Josephus, a Jewish historian who lived in the first century, also confirms the fact that the books of the Old Testament were originally twenty-two in number:

"We have not a countless number of books, discordant and arranged against each other; but only two and twenty books, containing the history of every age, which are justly accredited as divine."
– Josephus, Against Apion 1.8 line 38

How To Study Your Bible

Old Testament Comparison Chart

Today's Old Testament

Pentatuech (The Law)
1. Genesis
2. Exodus
3. Leviticus
4. Numbers
5. Deuteronomy

Historical Books
6. Joshua
7. Judges
8. Ruth
9. 1 Samuel
10. 2 Samuel
11. 1 Kings
12. 2 Kings
13. 1 Chronicles
14. 2 Chronicles
15. Ezra
16. Nehemiah
17. Esther

Wisdom Books
18. Job
19. Psalms
20. Proverbs
21. Ecclesiastes
22. Song of Solomon

Major Prophets
23. Isaiah
24. Jeremiah
25. Lamentations
26. Ezekiel
27. Daniel

Minor Prophets
28. Hosea
29. Joel
30. Amos
31. Obadiah
32. Jonah
33. Michah
34. Nahum
35. Habakkuk
36. Zephaniah
37. Haggai
38. Zechariah
39. Malachi

Original Old Testament

Torah (The Law)
1. Genesis
2. Exodus
3. Leviticus
4. Numbers
5. Deuteronomy

The Prophets

Former Prophets
6. Joshua-Judges
7. Book of Kingdoms
    (1 & 2 Samuel, 1 & 2 Kings combined)

Latter Prophets
8. Isaiah
9. Jeremiah
10. Ezekiel

Minor Prophets
11. Book of the Twelve
    (Hosea, Joel, Amos, Obadiah, Jonah, Micah, Nahum, Habakkuk, Zephaniah, Haggai, Zechariah, Malachi)

The Writings
12. Psalms
13. Proverbs
14. Job
15. Song of Solomon
16. Ruth
17. Lamentations
18. Ecclesiastes
19. Esther
20. Daniel
21. Ezra-Nehemiah
22. Chronicles
    (1 & 2 Chronicles combined)

90

New Testament Comparison Chart

Today's New Testament	Original New Testament
Gospels and Acts	**Gospels and Acts**
1. Matthew	1. Matthew
2. Mark	2. Mark
3. Luke	3. Luke
4. John	4. John
5. Acts	5. Acts
Pauline Epistles	**General Epistles**
6. Romans	6. James
7. 1 Corinthians	7. 1 Peter
8. 2 Corinthians	8. 2 Peter
9. Galatians	9. 1 John
10. Ephesians	10. 2 John
11. Philippians	11. 3 John
12. Colossians	12. Jude
13. 1 Thessalonians	
14. 2 Thessalonians	**Pauline Epistles**
15. 1 Timothy	13. Romans
16. 2 Timothy	14. 1 Corinthians
17. Titus	15. 2 Corinthians
18. Philemon	16. Galatians
	17. Ephesians
General Epistles	18. Philippians
19. Hebrews	19. Colossians
20. James	20. 1 Thessalonians
21. 1 Peter	21. 2 Thessalonians
22. 2 Peter	22. Hebrews
23 1 John	23. 1 Timothy
24. 2 John	24. 2 Timothy
25. 3 John	25. Titus
26. Jude	26. Philemon
Prophecy	**Prophecy**
27. Revelation	27. Revelation

The Original New Testament

The original New Testament manuscripts were also arranged in a different order in the beginning:

I. The Historical Books (the Gospels and Acts)
II. The General Epistles (James to Jude)
III. The Pauline Epistles (Romans to Hebrews, but with Hebrews in the 10th place instead of after Philemon)
IV. The Book of Revelation

The Gospels and Acts came first, as one would expect, but they were followed by the General Epistles. The General Epistles are also sometimes called the Catholic Epistles, because the word "catholic" means "general" or "universal." At the time these epistles were named, there was no Roman Catholic Church yet. The term Catholic Epistles simply refers to those letters which were written to the general church, the church universal, and their name is unrelated to Roman Catholicism as it exists today.

The Pauline Epistles originally came after the General Epistles, once again following the biblical principle of eldership. Peter and John were among the original Twelve Apostles of Jesus, while James and Jude were half-brothers of Jesus. James and Jude were born to Mary and Joseph following Jesus' birth (Matthew 13:55), and they became disciples of Jesus following His resurrection. All four of these men were followers of Christ long before Paul became a Christian on his ride to Damascus (Acts 9:1-19).

The ordering of the Pauline Epistles matches that of our Bibles today, but with one major variation. While modern translations place the Book of Hebrews at the beginning of the General Epistles, the original position of Hebrews was at the end of Paul's letters to his churches, between 2 Thessalonians and 1 Timothy. As with our Bible today, the original New Testament closed with the Book of Revelation.

We know this is the proper positioning of the New Testament books because all four of the earliest manuscripts that we have access to today all position them in that order. These four codices are the *Vaticanus,* the *Sinaiticus,* the *Alexandrinus,* and the *Ephraem.* Since there is no doubt among professional Bible scholars that the General Epistles belong before the Pauline Epistles, why has this pattern been abandoned by all of our modern translators?

Once again, they are following the arbitrary arrangement of the Latin Vulgate translation by Jerome, who in the early 5th century placed the letters of the Apostle Paul ahead of the seven General Epistles, which at that time were considered to be too "Jewish." For the same reason, Jerome moved Hebrews from its original position of 10th among the Pauline Epistles all the way to the back of the list behind Philemon.

In the eyes of Jerome this arrangement had the advantage of exalting the position of Paul (the Apostle to the Gentiles) to a place of authority above those Jewish apostles who were commissioned to preach to the Jews. Additionally, this radical decision to place Paul's letters ahead of the seven General Epistles in his Latin Vulgate just happened to put the Book of Romans (and by extension the city of Rome) into the first ranking position among the epistles, before the Jewish apostolic authors, and ahead of the city of Jerusalem.

The decision to arrange the New Testament books in this order was done entirely for political reasons, to exalt the Gentile section of the Christian Church, and the city of Rome in particular.

It has absolutely no basis in the majority of the early Greek manuscripts of the New Testament. Noted Bible scholar E.W. Bullinger had this to say about the arrangement of Jerome:

"Our English Bibles follow the order as given in the Latin Vulgate. This order, therefore, depends on the arbitrary judgment of one man, Jerome (A.D. 382–429). All theories based on this order rest on human authority, and are thus without any true foundation."
- Companion Bible, Appendix 95

The Latin Vulgate Bible was a highly successful attempt by Jerome to exalt the position of the western Latin Church over the eastern Greek churches, and to put the Church of Rome ahead of all the other major Patriarchal city churches in Christendom at the time.

This conclusion is confirmed by all of the textual scholarship of the last century, which proved out the true order of the New Testament books from the four oldest manuscripts as they were discovered.

God's Original Bible

Why does it matter how the books of the Bible were originally laid out? When the original arrangement of the Old and New Testament books are taken together, a design emerges, revealing a symmetrical balance between the books of the Bible that is truly inspiring. Note that the Bible was originally comprised of 22 books in the Old Testament and 27 books in the New Testament, for a total of 49 books. 49 is the product of 7 times 7, and seven is the number symbolizing divine completion in the Scriptures.

Jesus also taught that there were three divisions in the Old Testament: 1) the Law of Moses, 2) the Prophets, and 3) the Psalms (or, the Writings). When we add the four divisions of the New Testament, which are as follows: 4) the Historical Books of the Gospels and Acts, 5) the seven General Epistles, 6) the fourteen (2 x 7) Pauline Epistles, and 7) the Book of Revelation, we have a total of seven divisions which make up the entire Bible.

Furthermore, Jesus Christ is placed directly in the center of God's original biblical order. In this original arrangement of the Bible, the four Gospels and the Book of Acts are book-ended by the 22 books of the Old Testament before, and the 22 remaining New Testament books that follow it. In this arrangement, the Gospel of Luke, which describes the Incarnation of Christ in greatest detail, occupies the position at the very center of the Bible (the 25th book).

In other words, the central part of the Bible would have been those books covering the life of Jesus Christ and

His activity in the early Church. This should be an obvious marker to us, but we have lost it as a result of the man-inspired reorganization of the Bible as we have it today.

As a final confirmation of this numerical symbolism, we know that the number 6 represents the number of man in the Bible. Adam was created on the 6th day, and multiples of 6 are found throughout the Bible, all associated with man. The last one, 666, the Mark of the Beast, is even called "the number of a man" (Revelation 13:18).

Today our Bible has 66 books, which based on the Bible's own numerical symbolism, gives off the impression that it is a human book, and not divine. This is precisely what the devil wants the world to believe, and this number of 66 books has not gone unnoticed by theologically educated atheists who are critics of the Bible.

This number of books was also perceived as a serious image problem by the Roman Catholic Church who, refusing to abandon the order of books in the Latin Vulgate, instead officially accepted 11 of the 14 apocryphal books into their new canon of Scripture at the Council of Trent in the 16th century.

This action was done to bring the total number of books in their Bible to 77, a much more appealing symbolic number, but in reality it further corrupted the Bible by importing 11 books that were never considered to be divinely inspired prior to the Council of Trent.

As with any Bible subject, one can go to extremes with biblical numerology, but in this case the numerical symbolism is absolutely undeniable. If the original Bible arrangement had been kept, our Bibles today would have 49 books (7 times 7), making it easily identifiable as God's true holy book.

Unfortunately, it is unlikely that a Bible with the books in their proper order will be published today. The current arrangement is just too ingrained in our history and culture. While the majority of Bible scholars would likely support such an effort, most Christians who are unaware of these issues with the Bible would probably be highly resistant to such changes, which they would perceive as unnecessarily radical and needlessly innovative.

Furthermore, Christian publishers probably won't make the attempt to develop such a Bible, because it is unlikely they would gain their money back from the commercial venture, much less make any reasonable profit. Perhaps, in the days to come, emerging communication technologies such as print-on-demand or crowd-funding will make the publication of such a Bible more viable.

Bible Study Tools #5
Bible Dictionaries, Encyclopedias, Lexicons, and Topical Bibles

While parallel Bibles and study Bibles can be very helpful in determining the meaning of a Bible verse, as a student of the Bible there will be times when you will want to cast a wider net. For example, rather than focusing on a particular word or Bible verse, you might want to find out more on a certain Bible subject in general. The best tools for that purpose are Bible dictionaries, lexicons, and topical Bibles.

Bible Dictionaries and Bible Encyclopedias

Bible dictionaries are similar to regular dictionaries, but they are focused on Bible topics. A Bible encyclopedia is an expanded Bible dictionary, with longer articles on each topic instead of just a short definition. Both Bible dictionaries and Bible encyclopedias usually contain references you can look up in your Bible.

Bible dictionaries and encyclopedias explain many words, topics, customs and traditions found in the Bible, and they contain a wealth of historical, geographical, cultural and archeological information. Bible dictionaries also contain short biographies of major Bible characters.

Lexicons

Bible lexicons give the definitions of biblical Greek and Hebrew words that are found in the original languages of the New Testament and Old Testament. Lexicons help in understanding the origins and root meanings within the ancient language, and also provide the context and cultural meaning as intended by the authors.

Essentially, the Greek and Hebrew dictionaries in the back of Strong's Concordance are mini-lexicons, but a true lexicon will provide much more detailed and extensive information. Nevertheless, most lexicons make use of Strong's reference numbers, making it much easier to obtain a detailed understanding of the Hebrew and Greek language as it is used in the Bible. *Vine's Expository Dictionary of New Testament Words* (usually just called Vine's) is an example of an accessible Greek lexicon.

Topical Bibles

A Topical Bible is similar to a concordance, but instead of categorizing verses by word, they are categorized by topic. For example, looking up the topic of "faith," you might find verses listed where the word "faith" doesn't appear in the verse, but the word "believe" or "trust" does. The most popular topical Bibles are *Nave's Topical Bible* and *The Treasury of Scriptural Knowledge*.

Topical Bibles are different from Bible dictionaries or encyclopedias, because rather than give the definition of a Bible word, they provide a list of Bible verses related to that word. They can also include sections on topics that don't actually appear in the Bible by name. As an example, the word "Trinity" doesn't appear anywhere in the Bible itself, but because it is such an important Christian doctrine, there are 83 references to it in *Nave's Topical Bible.*

Bible Study Method #5
Topical Studies

A topical study is an in-depth study of a particular Bible topic, either through a single book, the Old or New Testament, or the entire Bible. The subject of your topical study can be almost anything you can think of that's in the Bible. The Topical Method is important for these reasons:

1) It enables us to study the Word of God systematically, logically, and in an orderly manner.

2) It gives us a proper perspective and balance regarding biblical truth. We get to see the whole of a biblical teaching.

3) It allows us to study subjects that are of particular interest to us.

4) It enables us to study the great doctrines of the Bible.

5) It lends itself to good and lively discussions. The results of a topical study are always easy to share with others.

6) It allows us variety in our personal Bible study.

Once you have a topic you want to study, make a list of questions you have about that topic. For example, if you were studying angels you might ask:

What do angels look like?
What do angels do?
How should we relate to angels?

All topical studies begin as word studies, but they can turn into massive verse studies, so proficiency in both of these Bible study methods will serve you well with topical studies. Here are the steps to a profitable topical study:

Step 1 – Find the Strong's reference number for the word

If I wanted to do an in-depth study on faith in the

New Testament, the first thing I would do is look it up in Strong's Concordance, where I would find that it is the word *pistis* in Greek (G4202).

Step 2 – Find all the Bible verses using that word

Next I would look up all the English words translated from that word and make a list of all the Bible verses that contain the word *pistis* (G4202), either by typing them out or copying them onto a document on the computer.

Typing them by hand is a good way to ingrain each verse in your mind, but if it's a word like *pistis* that has a lot of entries, this may not be practical.

Step 3 – Analyze each verse

Using the Verse Study method, make some notes about what you find in each verse. It can be helpful at this stage to write each verse on an index card. This step may take some time if there are a lot of verses related to your topic, but don't be lazy. It's very important that your verse analysis is thorough.

Step 4 – Sort the verses

Categorize verses that naturally complement each other and group them together on a separate sheet of paper. If you are using index cards as suggested, you can simply move the verse cards around into their appropriate groups. Larger sticky notes are also good to use for this step.

Step 5 – Define your sub-topics

Using each category as a subject heading, logically arrange the groups of Scriptures into an outline. This will make it easier for you to remember and will also make it easier to communicate to others.

Step 6 – Consult reference materials

At this point you've squeezed all you can out of these verses, so check the topical Bible study tools mentioned in this chapter to look for any further insights. It's always best to do your own analysis before consulting any reference materials. Even if you find something that's already covered in those books, the exercise of discovering it on your own will be very helpful to your Bible study career over the long term.

Step 7 – Apply what you've learned

Conclude your study with a practical application you can put to use in your own life. Write a brief paragraph summary of what you discovered in your topical study, and list the ways you can immediately apply your findings to your daily life.

Following Up

Due to the way Bible verses are sorted out in a topical study, it can be very easy to take things out of context, so be systematic. Don't try to study the Bible in a haphazard, undisciplined manner. When you make your list of all the things related to your topic, make it as comprehensive and complete as possible. Then take up these sub-topics one at a time, studying them in a systematic and logical order.

Take the time to be thorough. As much as possible, find and study every single verse you can that relates to the topic. The only way to know everything God has said on a particular subject is to go through the entire Bible and find all the passages related to that topic. Use your concordance to help you do this.

Finally, be exact. Try to get the exact meaning of every verse you study. Be sure to examine the context of each verse to avoid possible misinterpretation. The biggest mistake you must avoid is taking a verse out of its context, because doing so could lead to inaccurate conclusions in your topical study.

Summary

The Bible as we have it today does not follow the layout of the original Old and New Testament manuscripts. Understanding how the books of the Bible were originally arranged can inspire us and also help us to have a better sense of the story of the Bible.

A Concordance can help you study Bible words, and parallel Bibles and study Bibles can assist you in your study of Bible verses. When it comes to studying Bible topics, Bible dictionaries and encyclopedias, lexicons, and topical Bibles can be very helpful.

Topical Bible studies are based on the foundation of word and verse studies. Using a topical study, you can discover everything the Bible has to say on a particular subject. The key to a successful topical study is to be very thorough, systematic, and exacting so that you can avoid the mistake of taking the Bible verses you're studying out of their proper context.

By now you should be starting to feel truly empowered as a Bible student in your own right. We will always need Pastors and other anointed ministers to speak the Word into our lives, but how exciting is it for you to not be dependent on any other person when it comes to understanding the Scriptures? How awesome is it to be able to mine the nuggets of truth from God's Word on your own?

Chapter 5 Discussion Questions

1. Why is it important to be familiar with the original layout of the Bible?

2. What were the three main divisions of the original Hebrew Old Testament, in order?

3. What is meant by the principle of eldership, and how did that impact the formation of the original Old Testament?

4. What is the difference between the Former Prophets, the Latter Prophets, and the Minor Prophets?

5. Define the term "catholic" as it relates to the General Epistles in the New Testament.

6. Based on what you've learned about the Latin Vulgate, what was Jerome's motivation for rearranging the New Testament books into the order we still use today?

7. How was the numbering of the books in the original layout of the Bible spiritually symbolic?

8. Bible Lexicons define words taken from the original manuscripts of what two biblical languages?

9. How does a Topical Bible differ from a Concordance?

10. What are some benefits of a Topical study?

11. When you're doing a Topical Bible study, why is it important to keep in mind the context of each verse?

Chapter 6

Characters In Context
Discovering the History of the Bible

*I have stored your word up in my heart, that
I might not sin against you. – Psalm 119:11*

Now that we know something about the story theme of the Bible and we have been introduced to the original layout of the Bible, the next obvious question is how did the assembly of the books of the Bible originally come about? Who determined what would be included in the Canon (meaning the official list) of Scripture? To answer that, we must look deeper into the history of the Bible.

There are two basic theories regarding the interpretation of history. One theory states that history is the inevitable social evolutionary progression of the mass of humanity, and individual people really don't matter. The other theory of history believes individuals certainly do matter, and in fact, at critical moments in history the decisions that key people make, whether heroic or horrendous, can determine the course that history takes.

The Bible definitely emphasizes the heroic interpretation of history. In this chapter we will not be covering the origins of every individual book (who wrote it, when, and to what audience). With the Bible study skills you already have, you can start figuring those things out on your own. Instead we will be focusing on how the various books came together to form the Bible as a whole.

How We Got Our Bible

Knowing the chronological order of the story of the Bible, with the added insights drawn from knowing how the original biblical manuscripts were arranged, gives you a huge advantage with understanding how we got our Bible. If your starting premise is incorrect, your conclusions will always be flawed. However, if your starting premise is accurate, discovering the history of the Bible becomes an exercise of simply filling in the blanks.

The Torah

The Torah begins with the Book of Genesis, but when was Genesis written? This is a trick question, because Jesus said Moses wrote Genesis (Matthew 19:8, referring to Adam and Eve), yet there's no way Moses could have known about the events recorded in Genesis because they all took place hundreds of years before his lifetime.

As you go through Genesis, you'll repeatedly come across the phrase, *"These are the generations of..."* These are called *toledoths,* a Hebrew word which is translated "generations." Each *toledoth* verse closes the section of Genesis which precedes it, and also indicates who the author of that section of Genesis was. Technically, Genesis was written by each *toledoth* author, starting from the time of Eden with God Himself (Genesis 2:4a). Moses concluded the *toledoth* sequence with the start of his writings (Exodus 1:6).

Toledoth Divisions of Genesis

1. Generations of the Heavens & Earth (Genesis 1:1-2:4a)

2. Generations of Adam (Genesis 2:4b-5:1a)

3. Generations of Noah (Genesis 5:1b-6:9a)

4. Generations of Shem, Ham, and Japheth (Genesis 6:9b-10:1)

5. Generations of Shem (Genesis 10:2-11:10a)

6. Generations of Terah (Genesis 11:10b-11:27a)

7. Generations of Isaac (Genesis 11:27b-25:19a)

8. Generations of Ishmael, through Isaac (Genesis 25:12-25:18)

9. Generations of Jacob (Genesis 25:19b-37:2a)

10. Generations of Esau, through Jacob (Genesis 36:1-36:43)

11. Generations of the Sons of Israel (Genesis 37:2b-Exodus 1:6)

Moses edited and collated Genesis into a single book and then started writing the rest of the Torah from Exodus through Deuteronomy. These writings included the Law given to Moses by God on Mount Sinai, as well as the historical events that occurred during Israel's years of wandering in the wilderness, all of which Moses lived through.

These writings by Moses came together to form the Torah. These books were so revered by the people of Israel, that after his death they were preserved with the greatest of care and attention.

The Prophets

The writings of the Prophets were added according to the chronological order of when these prophets carried out their ministries. Therefore, the Book of Joshua+Judges, which gives the history of the time when Israel had no king, is placed before the Book of the Kingdoms (our Samuel and Kings), which covers Israel's monarchy period.

Among the Former Prophets, Joshua+Judges was highly honored as the link between the Torah and everything else that followed. The Book of Kingdoms follows in historical order, mainly focusing on the reigns of seven rulers: Samuel, Saul, David, Solomon, Hezekiah, Josiah, and Jehoiachin.

The second section of the Prophets, the Major Prophets, is arranged in an identical way. Isaiah delivered his prophecies about the middle of the 8th century B.C. Jeremiah later began his prophetic ministry about 627 B.C. Even later, Ezekiel prophesied in about 592 B.C.

The third section of the Prophets also follows a chronological format. Not all of the twelve books within the Minor Prophets give a precise dating within their text, but we can still place them in a reasonably certain order by following the biblical principle of eldership, and based on the chronological references found in each of these 12 documents.

The easiest way to observe this is to start with Malachi, the last of the Book of the Twelve, and work back to Hosea. The historical context clues that are revealed, even when precise dates are not given, provide a good basis for concluding that each document, going backward from 12 to 1, is later than the one before it.

The Writings

The last major section of the original Old Testament begins with the Book of Psalms and ends with the Chronicles. All of these writings share a common theme of royalty. Psalms was written primarily by King David, while the Proverbs were written mainly by his son, King Solomon. Next in The Writings comes the Book of Job, who was also described as a king representing royalty (Job 29:25).

The next five books in The Writings are notable for their feminine nature, yet they still follow the royal theme. Song of Solomon is about a woman who wishes to be courted by King Solomon, and the "daughters of Jerusalem" are addressed several times. Ruth is unmistakably about the House of David's "Queen Mother," giving King David's early genealogical history. Next is Lamentations, in which Jeremiah writes about the destruction of Jerusalem, personifying her as the "Mother City" weeping over her dead children.

The next book is Ecclesiastes, and its Hebrew title is *Qoheleth*, a feminine word meaning "congregation of women." The Court of the Women was a place where female Israelites congregated in the Temple. King Solomon wrote this book to that audience, and in the context of the title he identifies himself as the "Teacher of the Assembled Women." After Ecclesiastes is the Book of Esther, a book written about a woman and for women. Esther was Queen of Persia, once again clearly following the royal theme of The Writings.

Following Esther is Daniel, another book of "royal" character. Daniel's visions concerned the history of world rulers, from Nebuchadnezzar of Babylon until the appearance of the Kingdom of God on Earth. Daniel himself was also a royal descendant of King David (Daniel 1:3).

The next book in the order is Ezra+Nehemiah, which was counted as one book by the Jews. Ezra was the person responsible for reestablishing the official government of God in Jerusalem after the Babylonian captivity. His partner in ministry was Nehemiah, who was also of royal blood, because only those who could trace their ancestry back to David were eligible to become King (see Nehemiah 6:6-7).

Ezra was a priest who led the way in resuming worship at the Temple in Jerusalem, while Nehemiah was the person predominantly responsible for setting up the government of Judah when the exiles returned from Babylon to Jerusalem. Ezra was the one who collected the divine library of books that would ultimately form the Old Testament in its entirety. The 17th century Rabbi Humphrey Prideaux stated of Ezra the priest:

"He (Ezra) collected together all the books of which the Holy Scriptures did then consist, and disposed them in their proper order, and settled the canon of Scripture for his time. These books he divided into three parts: first, the Law; secondly, the Prophets; and thirdly, the Ketubim or

Hagiographa, i.e. <u>the Holy Writings</u>; which division our Savior himself takes notice of in Luke 24:44." - Connection of the Old and New Testaments, pp.318–319

There is another early historical reference to the completion of the original Old Testament. The Jewish priestly rulers of the Maccabean family near the end of the 2nd century B.C. recognized that the canon of the Old Testament was completed about three hundred years earlier.

One of the books written about the history of these Maccabean kings is called 2 Maccabees, and while we do not receive it as inspired Scripture, it is a good historical source, similar to the writings of Josephus. 2 Maccabees clearly states that it was in the time of Ezra and Nehemiah when the canon of the Old Testament was established:

"Solomon also kept the eight days. The same thing was related also in the records and memoirs about Nehemiah, that he founded a library and collected the books about <u>the kings</u>, and <u>the prophets</u>, and <u>the works of David, and royal letters</u> about sacred gifts." - 2 Maccabees 2:12–15

Here we have historical evidence not only that Nehemiah built a library and collected the sacred books of the Old Testament, but as early as the 2nd century BC the complete Old Testament in its original form was widely recognized and accepted. In the quotation above, "the kings, and the prophets" clearly points to the second major division of The Prophets, and "the works of David, and royal letters" is an unmistakable reference to the third division, The Writings.

Finally, we have the Book of Chronicles (our 1 and 2 Chronicles), which was written in the time of Nehemiah. It reviews the history of Israel and focuses on the establishment of Jerusalem and the family of David as the only legitimate rulers for God's divine government upon the Earth.

Chronicles also mentions many other ancient historical books (1 Chronicles 27:24, 29:29; 2 Chronicles 9:29, 13:22, 20:34, 24:27, and 33:19). These are easily accounted for when we recall the library of Nehemiah, who was also a high official within the Persian Empire and would have had access to these works. Taken together, these chronological factors determined the placement of the Old Testament books. They are significant, as they reveal a deliberate design which inspired Ezra and his priests.

The New Testament

In chronological terms, the first New Testament books written were the epistles, which were sent out to the various churches scattered throughout the Roman Empire. The writing of the Gospels and Acts came later. The primary reason the original New Testament manuscripts have the General Epistles ahead of the Pauline Epistles is because their authors are honored as elders above the Apostle Paul.

The writers of the General Epistles were the Apostles James, Peter, John and Jude. All four of these men personally heard the teachings of Jesus when He ministered in Galilee and Judea, and they were anointed to preach the Gospel well before the day when Paul was saved on the road to Damascus. Paul himself recognized these men as his elders when he stated they were ministers *"before me"* (Galatians 1:17) and referred to himself as *"the least of the apostles"* (I Corinthians 15:9).

As the Gospel spread, false doctrines also spread. The epistles were written to combat these erroneous teachings, but more was needed. The solution was the writing of the Gospels, the first of which were written by John in Ephesus and Matthew in Antioch of Syria (though not all Bible scholars accept this order).

Both Peter and Paul also saw a need for an accurate accounting of the life of Christ, and this was a project that consumed both of them in the months leading up to their deaths. Peter knew he would be dying soon, so he wrote to his followers saying:

> **And I will make every effort so that after my departure you may be able <u>at any time</u> to recall these things. – 2 Peter 1:15**

Mark was associated with Peter at this time in his ministry (1 Peter 5:13), and he composed his Gospel based on Peter's eyewitness testimony (2 Peter 1:16). Peter also recognized the apostolic authority of Paul, going so far as to refer to Paul's letters as Holy Scripture.

> **And count the patience of our Lord as salvation, just as our beloved brother Paul <u>also wrote to you according to the wisdom given him, as he does in all his letters</u> when he speaks in them of these matters. There are some things in them**

that are hard to understand, which the ignorant and unstable twist to their own destruction, <u>as they do the other Scriptures</u>. – 2 Peter 3:15-16

The writers of the General Epistles were the apostles James, Peter, John and Jude. All four of these men personally heard the teachings of Jesus. Paul also considered himself to have the authority to write Holy Scripture. At the close of his Epistle to the Romans there is an interesting passage in which Paul said that his writings concerning the message of Christ were to be acknowledged as "the prophetic writings." This meant that Paul himself thought he was writing sacred Scriptures. Note the context of Paul's belief:

Now to him who is able to strengthen you <u>according to my gospel</u> and the preaching of Jesus Christ, <u>according to the revelation of the mystery</u> that was kept secret for long ages but has <u>now been disclosed</u> and <u>through the prophetic writings</u> has been made known to all nations, according to the command of the eternal God, to bring about the obedience of faith - to the only wise God be glory forevermore through Jesus Christ! Amen. - Romans 16:25-27

Luke was Paul's faithful companion until the end of Paul's life, and Paul's influence can be easily detected in the two companion volumes of Luke's writings, the Gospel of Luke and the Acts of the Apostles. Apparently, there were many others who were trying to get in on the act of writing about Jesus' life and ministry, but Luke understood that the true purpose of the Gospels was to give confidence to those who believed.

Inasmuch as <u>many have undertaken to compile a narrative</u> of the things that have been accomplished among us, just as those who from the beginning were eyewitnesses and ministers of the word have delivered them to us, it seemed good to me also, having followed all things closely for some time past, <u>to write an orderly account</u> for you, most excellent Theophilus, <u>that you may have certainty concerning the things you have been taught</u>.
   – Luke 1:1-4

With the deaths of Peter in A.D. 66 and Paul in A.D. 67, it was left to John to compile these various writings into the original manuscript of the New Testament. John was a priest prior to his association with John the Baptist. Later he left John the Baptist to follow Jesus the Messiah (see John 1:35-37, where the two disciples of John the Baptist were Peter's brother Andrew, and John, the Gospel author).

This is further proven by the fact that during the crucifixion John was able to walk right into the priests' quarters and was known by Caiaphas (John 18:15, 16). As both a priest and an apostle, John was designated to become the "voice" of the entire church.

That which was from the beginning, which <u>we</u> have heard, which <u>we</u> have seen with our eyes, which <u>we</u> looked upon and have touched with <u>our</u> hands, concerning the word of life - the life was made manifest, and <u>we</u> have seen it, and testify to it and proclaim to you the eternal life, which was with the Father and was made manifest

to us - that which we have seen and heard we proclaim also to you, so that you too may have fellowship with us; and indeed our fellowship is with the Father and with his Son Jesus Christ. And we are writing these things so that our joy may be complete. - 1 John 1:1-4

It's such an interesting story that we could easily fill another ten books with the details of how the Bible came together in the first century, but there is only space to summarize it here. The main point, contrary to the assertions of modern Bible critics, is that all of the books of Scripture were written and collated into a unified Bible before the end of the 1st century A.D. With the death of the Apostle John, the writing of the New Testament canon was closed, and the Holy Scriptures were complete.

Bible Study Tools #6
Bible Commentaries and Bible Handbooks

In the past couple of chapters as we've talked about various issues regarding the Bible, the role of Bible scholars has been mentioned. As a student of the Bible, wouldn't it be nice if you knew a few of these Bible scholars personally so you could pick their brains? Or better still, what if they were available to you when you had a question, at any time of the day or night? Bible commentaries and Bible handbooks, written by some of these very scholars, are the next best thing.

Bible Commentaries

A Bible Commentary is a scholarly collection of explanatory notes containing Scriptural interpretations, similar to the notes which can be found in a study Bible. The purpose of a commentary is to explain and interpret the meaning of a Bible passage, and the author's comments follow the normal order of the Scriptures.

The information found in a commentary is usually more extensive and in-depth than that which one would find in a study Bible. In a study Bible the notes are together with the Scriptures, but in commentaries the comments are always contained within a separate book or set of books.

Commentaries come in all shapes and sizes, from one volume editions to multi-volume series. Since these books are written by Biblical scholars, they can be extremely interesting reading, helping Bible students gain insights by pointing out connections between Scripture passages which they might have missed otherwise. However, sometimes the scholarly language can make for very dry reading. Examples of good Bible commentaries include the famous *Matthew Henry's Commentary* and the *Barclay's Daily Study Bible* series.

The same cautions that apply to Study Bibles also apply to commentaries. While Bible commentaries are very interesting, remember that they are written by fallible men who cannot help but inject their own opinions and pet doctrines into the text. Also, you should always make it a point to do your own study of a Bible passage first, then consult the commentaries afterward. Otherwise you'll risk robbing yourself of the joy of self-discovery!

Bible Handbooks

A Bible handbook is a combination of a Bible encyclopedia and a Bible commentary, written in a very concise form. Like commentaries, the entries follow the order of the Scriptures instead of giving an alphabetical list of topics. They are useful for quick reference while reading through a book of the Bible. Some popular examples of Bible handbooks are *Haley's Bible Handbook* and the *Holman Bible Handbook.*

Bible Study Method #6
Character Studies

At the start of this chapter we discussed the two main theories of history, and how the teaching of the Bible aligns with the theory that whenever there is a turning point in history, specific individuals will always be present to make the key decisions that will determine which course history will take. Character studies allow you to evaluate these Bible personalities so you can draw lessons from their lives.

The Character Study method, sometimes called the Biographical Method, studies the life of a certain Bible character. Essentially it's a topical study in which the topic being studied is a person from the Bible.

The Bible portrays its characters very realistically.

Unlike the holy books of other religions, where the flaws and mistakes of its heroes are either downplayed or ignored, the Bible gives us the good, the bad, and the ugly.

We see David heroically killing Goliath, we see him committing adultery with Bathsheba, and we see him plotting to kill her husband Uriah after David got Bathsheba pregnant.

We see Peter working miracles and casting out devils in Jesus' name, we see him running away as Jesus is arrested at Gethsemane, and finally we find him cursing at a young girl as he warms himself around a fire outside the place where Jesus was on trial.

The Bible absolutely refuses to whitewash the flaws of its characters, and this radically honest portrayal is one of the things that makes Bible character studies so interesting.

Even though they lived hundreds or even thousands of years ago, people are basically the same. They all have similar needs, wants and desires, which is what makes studying Bible characters so beneficial. Paul wrote to the church at Corinth that God gave the stories of the Old Testament to us as examples.

Now these things happened to them as an example, but they were written down for our instruction, on whom the end of the ages has come. – 2 Corinthians 10:11

We can actually receive instruction from God as we

How To Study Your Bible

examine both the good and bad examples shown to us by the characters of the Bible. The steps of a character study are similar to a normal topical study, but with slight variations.

Step 1 – Find all the Bible verses for that Bible character

Trace out the Bible references for that particular person and, using either paper or index cards, make a list of every Bible verse in which that person is mentioned. It's very likely you'll find references in multiple books. For example, you'll find verses about King David in the writings of Samuel, the Psalms, and the Chronicles. A study of the life of Peter would include verses from all four Gospels.

Step 2 – Analyze each verse

Do this just as you would in a regular topical study, following the verse study method described in chapter 4. How much time this step takes depends on the number of verses involved. A character study of Moses will take much longer than a character study of Enoch, for example, because there are not as many verses that refer to Enoch. One thing you'll want to look at is the meaning of the name. In the Bible, the meaning of a character's name is always significant and can give you more insights into that character.

Step 3 – Sort the verses

After analyzing each Bible verse, divide the verses

into categories, but in this case the categories will usually be phases or events taken from the person's life. For example, a character study of David might divide the verses into David's childhood, when he was a warrior, and when he was King. A character study of Peter might be divided into events such as when Jesus called him to follow, the various Gospel events Peter was involved in, and Peter's career as an Apostle as portrayed in Acts and his two epistles.

Step 4 – Construct a timeline

If you're not quite sure how you should divide the verses into categories, sort the verses chronologically and create a timeline of the Bible character's life. Often when you do that, patterns will emerge, and the best way to sort the verses will become clearer. Making a timeline will also help you make new connections between the verses, especially if the material for that character is drawn from more than one book in the Bible.

Step 5 – List the Sins and the Wins

Remember that the reason you're getting to know this character is because God has given you information about this person's life so that you can receive instruction and learn from their example. If you're not going to apply the lessons you've learned from the character's life, then why are you even doing this? Take note of the character's attitudes and goals, and record the strengths and weaknesses that are revealed. Look for good examples you can emulate, and be on the lookout for mistakes they made that you can avoid in your own life.

How To Study Your Bible

How To Study Your Bible

Step 6 – Look for key relationships

The reason people are so interesting to watch is because of the relationships they form with each other, and the same holds true for Bible characters. As you examine the lives of the characters you're studying, look for people in their lives who were influential for any reason, and also look for people whom the Bible character may have influenced. Often these relationships will branch out into exciting new character studies.

Step 7 – Watch out for name variations

Be aware of character name variations and multiple usages of names. For example, Isaiah is called Esaias in the New Testament because that's the Greek spelling of his name. Sometimes the same person goes by multiple names because at some point in the story his name was changed, such as Jacob being renamed Israel, Simon being renamed Peter, and Saul being renamed Paul. To get the full picture of these characters, you need to find all the Bible verses for each of the names in question.

Step 8 – Consult reference materials

Finally, after you've gathered all the information from the verses that you can on your own, consult various Bible commentaries to supplement your study efforts. Often you will find the commentators reveal insights and connections you may have missed, but you should still do the initial character study on your own in order to help strengthen your Bible student skillset.

Following Up

Once you've learned all about the Bible character's motives and actions, it will become much easier to get an accurate mental picture of his or her life. As you start getting deeper into Bible character studies, don't be surprised to find yourself getting emotionally attached to these Bible characters, sympathizing with some of their actions, while also intensely disliking some of the choices they make. This is a normal reaction, especially considering that you're going to be able to meet most of them one day.

Summary

The history of how we got our Bible largely follows the original layout of the Bible, which makes sense when you recognize the chronological flow of the original manuscript. From Moses to the time of Ezra and Nehemiah, God not only inspired the Holy Scriptures, but He also preserved them across all those centuries.

The New Testament largely started coming together as an apostolic reaction to heretical teachings that were cropping up in the churches. To combat these false doctrines, the Apostles wrote letters to their churches. The General Epistles were originally placed before the Pauline Epistles because the Jewish Apostles were elder to the Apostle Paul, a fact which Paul himself recognized. The Epistles were followed by the Gospels and Acts, which were intended by the Apostles to be the official record of the life and teachings of Christ and the early church.

These teachings are elaborated on in Bible commentaries, which can be read to assist the Bible student with interpreting and explaining the meaning of a particular Bible passage. The information contained within Bible commentaries is ordered according to the order of Scripture.

Similarly, Bible handbooks are a kind of combination between a commentary and a Bible encyclopedia, making them very useful for quick reference on a Bible topic. Yet, while Bible commentaries and handbooks can open up whole new vistas of biblical understanding to us, we must always remember that the thoughts and opinions they contain are those of fallible men.

The Bible character study method is a specialized form of topical study with a person from the Bible as the topic. Since the Bible records both the victories and the failures of its characters objectively, Bible character studies can be some of the most interesting and exciting studies you will perform.

The stories of the people in the Bible have been given to us by God as examples, which He uses to provide us with instruction. The steps of a Bible character study are slightly different from a regular topical study, but the benefits you can draw from them are almost limitless.

You're now at the halfway point of How To Study The Bible. In the upcoming chapters we're going to look at where our English Bible came from, and then we'll compare the King James Version to other English versions so that you'll be able to choose which Bible would be best for you.

Chapter 6 Discussion Questions

1. What is a *Toledoth?* Based on what you now know about *Toledoths,* how was Moses able to chronicle the life of Adam and Eve?

2. How were the books of the Prophets added to the original Hebrew manuscript?

3. The Writings are characterized by their representation of royalty and their feminine nature. Why is this significant?

4. Consider the phrase, "It's not what you say, but how you say it." How would being able to hear Jesus speak add to the value of His words? How would that affect the men who recorded those words?

5. The earliest New Testament writings were the Epistles. What was the main reason they were written? (page 113)

6. What is the value of studying a Bible passage on your own, prior to consulting a Bible Commentary?

7. What do you always need to remember when utilizing Bible Commentaries and Study Bibles?

8. A Bible Handbook is a combination of which two Bible study tools?

9. What is the purpose of a biography? How is this similar or different from the purpose of the Bible? How do the biographies of Bible heroes add to the story of the Bible?

Chapter 7

Bible Wars
How We Got Our English Bible

*Open my eyes, that I may behold wondrous
things out of your law. - Psalm 119:18*

In addition to various Bible study tools and methods, we've been learning about the Bible itself. First we learned the layout of the Bible as we have it today, including how to use the reference numbers for chapters and verses. Next, we discussed the story-arc of the Bible, and how all the individual Bible stories fit within that overall theme.

After that, we covered the original layout of the Bible, as it appeared in the earliest extant manuscripts, and we talked about why the order of the books was ultimately changed to the Bible that is in use today. Then we reviewed the history of the Bible, and how the various books within it came together to form both the Old and New Testaments.

Now we're going to take a look at how the Bible was translated into the English language. So many Christians are ignorant of how this came to be. The story of how the English Bible originated is an exciting story in its own right, one which you should know and understand. When you learn how the Bible came to be translated into English, it will give you a new level of appreciation for that sacred book you hold in your hands.

History of the English Bible

The transmission of the original Scriptures into the Hebrew and Greek occurred from about 1600 B.C. to 100 A.D. By the end of the 4th century A.D. the common language was no longer Greek. Instead, almost everyone spoke Latin, so the Scriptures weren't accessible to most Christians. Seeing the need for a Latin language Bible, Jerome started work on his Latin Vulgate edition, which he completed in 405 A.D.

Although he started with good intentions, we have already seen how Jerome's efforts were marred by his decision to reorder the books of the Bible in order to elevate the position of Rome over that of Jerusalem. Other translations were also created, so that by 500 A.D. the Bible had been translated into over 500 languages. However, by 600 A.D. these Bibles were restricted so that only one version was allowed: the Latin Vulgate.

At that time the only organized church was the Roman Catholic Church. There were no Protestant denominations yet, and the Great Schism, which was the division of the empire into the western Roman Church and the Eastern Orthodox Church, was still 450 years away. Rome was in complete control, and the Roman Catholic Church refused to allow the Bible to be made available in any language except Latin. Over the 200 years since the creation of the Latin Vulgate, Latin had fallen by the wayside, to be replaced with other languages. The Dark Ages had begun.

(Note: It is almost impossible to tell the story of how we got our English Bible without potentially offending our Roman Catholic and Anglican brothers and sisters in Christ. We must recognize that this history recounts the motivations and decisions of the Roman Church leadership of that period, and is not necessarily a reflection of Roman Catholic believers today. However, these abuses by the Roman Church at that time did provoke the start of the Reformation, which is what led to the eventual publication of the Bible in the English language.)

Only the priests were educated to understand Latin, so the common people were forced to accept Rome's interpretation of the Scriptures without question. This power corrupted the Church leadership, allowing them to deceive the masses and extort money from them due to their enforced ignorance. Possession of a non-Latin copy of the Bible was considered sacrilege and punishable by death.

This state of affairs continued for centuries until a tipping point was reached when Pope Leo X started a new practice called the "selling of indulgences" as yet another way to get money out of the people. He offered forgiveness of sins for a small amount of money, or for a larger contribution a person would be allowed to indulge in a continuous sinful lifestyle such as adultery without penalty.

The Roman Church also invented the doctrine of

"Purgatory" where the masses were encouraged to purchase salvation for the souls of their loved ones who had already died. The ignorant people were taught by Rome, "As soon as the coin in the coffer rings, the troubled soul from Purgatory springs!" Pope Leo X was quoted as saying, "The fable of Christ has been quite profitable to us!"

John Wycliffe

Known throughout Europe as a vocal opponent of the teachings of the Roman Church, Oxford professor and theologian John Wycliffe produced the first English language manuscripts in the 1380's. His Bible was a hand-written translation of the Latin Vulgate, which was the only source text available to him.

With the help of many faithful scribes, his followers produced dozens of English language copies of the Scriptures, earning him the enduring hatred of Rome. The Pope was so infuriated that the common people were gaining access to the Word of God that 44 years after Wycliffe's death he ordered Wycliffe's posthumous execution. Wycliffe's bones were dug up, crushed, burned, and scattered in the Severn River.

The Start of the Reformation

John Hus, a follower of Wycliffe, actively promoted Wycliffe's teachings that the people should oppose the abuses of the Roman Church and be allowed to read the Bible in their own language. In 1415 Hus was burned at the stake, with Wycliffe Bibles used as kindling for the fire. His last words were a prophecy: "In 100 years, God will raise up a man whose calls for reform cannot be suppressed."

In the 1440's Johann Gutenberg invented the printing press, and the first book ever printed was a Latin language Bible. The innovation of moveable type meant that Bibles and other books could be accurately reproduced in large quantities over a very short period of time. This new technology was the key to the success of the Reformation.

Fulfilling the prophecy of John Hus' last words, almost exactly 100 years later, Martin Luther nailed his famous 95 *Theses* (a list of 95 complaints concerning the false teachings and crimes of the Roman Catholic Church) onto the church door at Wittenberg in 1517. Luther would go on to translate the Bible into German. According to *Foxe's Book of Martyrs,* seven people were burned at the stake in England that same year for the criminal act of teaching their children to recite the Lord's Prayer in English instead of Latin.

William Tyndale

Referred to as the Captain of the Army of Reformers, William Tyndale was the spiritual leader of the Reformation in England. A scholar who was fluent in eight different languages, his genius was to combine the hand-written translation of Wycliffe with the invention of Gutenberg. Rumors of Tyndale's upcoming New Testament forced him to flee England in order to avoid the Inquisitors and bounty hunters who were sent to arrest him and stop his publishing project.

He worked with Martin Luther in Germany to become the first man ever to print the entire New Testament in English in 1525, and by the 1530's Tyndale New Testaments were being distributed throughout England. Church authorities confiscated and burned as many as they could, but many copies were successfully smuggled in, one even ending up in the bedroom of King Henry VIII.

Making the Word of God available in English to the people threatened the corrupt leadership of the Roman Church. If they couldn't restrict access to the Bible and believers were able to read it in their own language, then the contradictions between what the church was preaching and what God's Word actually said would soon become apparent. As the people began to challenge the Church's authority, Rome's income structure would collapse and the Roman Church would lose much of her political power.

Yet, the more they fought against the spread of the Tyndale New Testament, the more interested in it the people became, even though the penalty for being caught with one was death by burning at the stake. For 11 years, Tyndale's Bibles and other books streamed into England, hidden in sacks of flour and bales of cotton.

Tyndale's largest customer was the King's officers, who would purchase every copy they could so they could burn them, but Tyndale simply used that money to print more. William Tyndale was finally betrayed and captured, and was held in prison for 500 days, before being strangled and burned at the stake in 1536. His last words were, "Oh Lord, open the King of England's eyes!" It was a prayer that God would answer just three short years later in 1539.

Tyndale's Disciples

Myles Coverdale and John Rogers were loyal followers of Tyndale during the last six years of his life, and when he died they carried on with his ministry to print and distribute the English Bible. Coverdale finished translating the Old Testament into English for the first time, using Luther's German Bible and the Latin text as sources. In October 4, 1535, he printed the first complete Bible in the English language, known today as the Coverdale Bible.

John Rogers printed the second complete English Bible in 1537, but his Bible was the first to be translated directly from Hebrew and Greek, the original languages of the Bible. It was a combination of Tyndale's Pentateuch and New Testament, the Coverdale Bible, and some of Roger's own translation work. He printed it under the assumed name "Thomas Matthew," an alias that Tyndale had also used.

King Henry VIII

King Henry VIII became the first monarch to allow an English Bible to be funded and printed by the English government. He was guided by his lust, not a pure conscience, but God will often turn the motives of wicked men to His glory. King Henry, who had already executed two of his many wives, had asked the Pope to allow him to divorce his current wife so that he might marry his mistress, a request the Pope refused.

The King married his mistress anyway, at the same time renouncing Roman Catholicism and ending Rome's religious control in England. He declared himself the new head of the Church of England. This new branch of Christianity wasn't Roman Catholic, yet it wasn't truly Protestant either. It became known as the Anglican Church, and King Henry acted as its new "Pope." To further demonstrate his contempt toward Rome, his first spiteful act was to fund the printing of the first official English Bible.

This Bible came to be known as the "Great Bible" due to its very large size. In 1539, Myles Coverdale was hired by Thomas Cranmer, the Archbishop of Canterbury, to publish the Great Bible. A copy was sent to every church, chained to the pulpit, and a reader was assigned so that even the illiterate could hear God's Word in plain English. Just three years after his martyrdom, the dying prayer of Tyndale had been answered.

The Geneva Bible

After the death of King Henry VIII, King Edward the VI ascended the throne, and after his reign Queen Mary came to power. Known as "Bloody Mary," she was obsessed with returning England to the Roman Catholic Church. In 1555, she had John Rogers and Thomas Cranmer burned at the stake. During her reign she had many other reformers burned at the stake, causing hundreds of Protestant refugees to flee England for their lives, a period known as the Marian Exile.

The Church at Geneva, Switzerland, was very sympathetic to the Reformers, welcoming them and offering their city as a safe haven. They were led by Myles Coverdale and John Foxe (author of the famous *Foxe's Book of Martyrs*), and were joined by John Knox, a Reformer of the Scottish Church, and John Calvin, the great theologian.

Together they decided to produce a Bible which they could use to educate their families while they lived in exile from England. Their New Testament was finished in 1557, and the entire Bible was completed in 1560. It became known as the Geneva Bible, named after the city where it was created.

This Bible also included study notes by Calvin in the margins, making it the first true "study Bible" ever published. However, many of Calvin's study notes stridently opposed the institutional church, causing many ruling monarchs to look upon it unfavorably. With the end of Queen Mary's bloody reign, these Reformers were finally able to return to England.

The Anglican Church was now under the control of Queen Elizabeth I, and it tolerated the production of the Geneva Bible in England. By now, the Anglican Church's copies of the Great Bible were several decades old, and a new English version was desired, but one that would be less politically inflammatory than the Geneva Bible. In 1568, the Bishop's Bible was published. A revision of the Great Bible, it never gained much traction with the people, despite 19 editions being printed between 1568 and 1606. It simply couldn't compete with the Geneva Bible, which was a much more popular version.

Douay-Rheims

By the 1580's it became apparent to the Roman Church

that they had lost the fight to suppress English translations of the Word of God. The decision was made that if there were going to be English Bibles, then they would create a Roman Catholic translation and declare that to be the official version. The New Testament of this Catholic English Bible was produced in the city of Rheims, and the Old Testament was translated in the city of Douay. The combined Bible, finished in 1609, was called the Douay-Rheims version.

Yet it was a corrupted English translation, as it carried over all the errors of the Latin Vulgate, which was used as the source text. In 1589 Fulke's Refutation was published in England by Dr. Willam Fulke of Cambridge. Taken from the New Testament, Fulke printed side by side columns of the Bishop's Bible and the Rheims version, technically creating the first "parallel Bible," with the purpose of showing the errors contained in Rome's corrupted compromise of their official English version.

Nevertheless, the publication of the Douay-Rheims Bible was an open admission by the Roman Catholic Church that she had lost the battle against the Reformers over whether the Bible would only be read in Latin, or if it could be read in English as well. At the same time, the highly popular Geneva Bible was so politically controversial, due to the radical nature of Calvin's marginal study notes, that the rulers of England remained reluctant to fully endorse it.

So while English Bibles were finally available, there was still a need for an English version which would satisfy the people's hunger for an accurate translation of the Word of God, yet also meet the government's desire to encourage social and political stability.

This need was finally met when Queen Elizabeth I died, and Prince James VI of Scotland ascended the throne to become King James I of England. We will cover the King James Bible, along with many of the questions that surround it, in the next chapter.

The main point of going through this history in such detail is to make you aware of the high price that was paid so that you might enjoy your own English Bible. Men of God struggled against religious tyranny for almost 250 years to possess an English Bible. They suffered, bled, burned, and died that you might be able to hold a Bible in your hands written in your own language. Thank God for them, never forget their sacrifice, and treasure your Bible accordingly.

Bible Study Tools #7
Chronological Bibles, Bible Timelines, and Gospel Harmonies

The Bible study tools in this chapter all involve rearranging the Scriptures into a different order, making them easier to understand. After reviewing these Bible study tools, we'll look at the chronological Bible study method.

Chronological Bibles

Chronological Bibles contain the text of the entire Bible, but the Scriptures are rearranged into a chronological order. To give you an idea of what a chronological Bible is like, here is how one might begin:

In the beginning was the Word, and the Word was with God, and the Word was God. The same was in the beginning with God.
   - John 1:1, 2 (KJV)

Before the mountains were brought forth, or ever thou hadst formed the earth and the world, even from everlasting to everlasting, thou art God. - Psalm 90:2 (KJV)

In the beginning God created the heaven and the earth. - Genesis 1:1 (KJV)

The chronological order follows the narrative of the Biblical story, not the order of when the books were written. Two good examples are The *Reese Chronological Bible* and the *Chronological Study Bible.*

Bible Timelines and Genealogies

A timeline is a visual representation of a series of historical events. Bible timelines are a helpful tool for determining the order in which events took place, such as how long certain Bible figures lived, or what order certain kings reigned, for example. Bible Timelines can be found online and in most Christian book stores.

Bible Genealogies are another form of timeline, except that events are tracked by generations instead of by measuring units of time. Looking at a Bible family tree can bring out details and connections between Bible characters that might have otherwise been missed.

For example, one of King David's wisest advisors, Ahithophel, betrayed David during Absalom's rebellion (2 Samuel 15:12). How could such a wise man make such a terrible mistake? Bible genealogy reveals the answer: Ahithophel was Bathsheba's grandfather, and for years he had no doubt suppressed burning anger and resentment toward David for the murder of Uriah, Bathsheba's first husband. When Absalom called for him, temptation overcame him because of the bitterness he held inside.

Many connections made in the Bible are subtle and won't be detected with just a cursory reading, but with tools like Bible timelines and genealogies these links can be brought out, tying things together in a way that will increase both your understanding and your enjoyment of the Bible.

Gospel Harmonies

A Gospel Harmony is a study tool that attempts to compile multiple retellings of the same Gospel event into a single account. The first three Gospels, Matthew, Mark and Luke, record many of the same stories, but sometimes different details are given in each account. A few stories are also repeated in the Gospel of John.

A Harmony of the Gospels takes all of the events, teachings, and miracles from the Gospels and attempts to arrange them in a coherent order. This is necessary because the Gospel authors didn't always record the events of Jesus' life in chronological order for literary reasons. For example, Matthew was more concerned with communicating how Jesus fulfilled the Messianic prophecies of the Old Testament.

A harmony of the Resurrection story would analyze passages from Matthew 28:1-15, Mark 16:1-11, Luke 24:1-12, and John 20:1-18. Since the details of each of these accounts differ slightly from the others, a Bible Harmony can be used to attempt to resolve the apparent conflicts and demonstrate the unity of the story as a whole. By taking similar events from one or more of the Gospels, comparing them side by side, and then combining them into a unified account, new insights can be gained, and many supposed conflicts between the stories can be understood and resolved.

Sometimes when comparing two different Gospel Harmonies you will find they don't agree. This is due to differing opinions among Bible scholars as to how the harmonized events should be ordered. Don't put too much weight on the specific ordering, since it's usually impossible to tell which harmony is "correct." Remember that the Gospels were written to proclaim the "good news" and were never intended to be taken as strictly historical books.

The point of a Gospel harmony isn't for historical accuracy, but rather to compare and contrast different passages that describe the same event so that you can learn more about it. Since different Bible writers will emphasize different points, it can be very helpful to create a composite of the event from the different accounts. A Gospel Harmony is the Bible study tool that allows you to do this.

Bible Study Method #7
Chronological Studies

A chronological Bible study combines the topical study and the character study methods, studying the lives of Bible characters or Bible events in their historical order. This is a very helpful Bible study method for putting Bible passages in their proper context, and can be easily done using the tools described in the previous section.

An example of an interesting chronological Bible study could be listing out the events in the life of David, and then inserting individual Psalms into the chronology when they were written. This would allow you to see what was happening in David's life when he wrote each Psalm, and would also give you greater understanding into the Psalm itself.

Did you know that you can trace Jesus' family tree from Adam all the way to Jesus? This is yet another example of a chronological Bible study. When you start to understand how much revelation can be opened up to you with the chronological study method, combined with what you've already learned about how to do a character study, you'll find that all of those "begats" of the Bible genealogies suddenly become a lot more interesting!

Another example of a chronological Bible study could be taking the events of the life of Paul in the Book of Acts, and then inserting his Epistles into the Acts narrative at the time when they were written. This would help you to see where Paul was when he wrote each letter, and might help you to get more out of the content of those letters.

These are just a few examples of what you can discover with this Bible study method. Here are the steps so that you can perform your own chronological Bible studies:

1. Decide what event you want to study

This can be almost anything you want it to be. Do you have questions about how a particular set of circumstances came into being at the start of a Bible story? Are you curious about what causes led to what effects? Chronological studies are great for breaking down a complex series of events.

2. Determine the main Scripture passage for that event

What is the main Scripture passage where this Bible event is covered? Where in the Bible is the most material about your event found? This is where you will want to begin.

3. Find other Scripture passages that also touch on that event

What other passages in the Bible touch on that same event? These are other locations where material concerning the event you are studying can be found.

4. Create a timeline of the pieces that make up the event

Using your main Scripture passage as the foundation, insert pieces from the other passages where they best fit. This could be more detailed information about what's already in the main passage, or new information that the first passage doesn't contain. When you've blended all the pieces together in their correct order, then you will have a complete picture of that Bible event.

5. What Bible characters are associated with that event?

Look at the characters that are involved with this Bible event. What was each character's point of view about what happened? What motivated each character in the story to do what they did? What were their goals, or what was each character trying to achieve? What key choices were made by any of the characters that affected the course of events in the story?

6. Examine the What If's

Now think about what could have happened differently in the story. What should have happened vs. what actually did happen? What if certain characters had made different choices? In what ways might better choices have caused a different outcome? This is useful because it allows you to learn from the mistakes made by characters in the Bible, instead of having to learn them for yourself.

7. Identify the life lessons you can apply

This is the most important step. It's not enough just to be proud of yourself for figuring out all of the intricacies of a particular Bible event. You have to be able to pull lessons out of it which you can then apply to your own life. Can you relate to what any of the characters thought, said or did? What can you learn from their example? What mistakes did they make that you could avoid? What did they do right that you could emulate in your life?

Following Up

The chronological study method combines many of the study methods you've learned up to this point, and it can be one of the most effective ways to really get a feel for the flow of a series of Bible events. You won't always need to go to the lengths of a full chronological study to find the answers to your questions, but you will find that these types of Bible studies will almost always branch off into other exciting studies, which will allow you to build up your understanding of the Bible more and more.

Summary

When the books of the Bible were all put together everyone still spoke Greek, but by the late 4th century Greek was falling by the wayside, having been replaced by Latin. Jerome met the need for a Latin Bible with his Vulgate edition, which remained the only Bible for the next 1000 years, despite the fact that the Latin language fell out of general usage later on.

During the Reformation, Germans and Englishmen sought to create a Bible translation in their own languages. Thanks to the invention of the printing press, these new Bibles could be easily mass produced and distributed. The story of how our English Bible came into being is both inspiring and sobering, and we should be very grateful to the men who sacrificed so much so that we could have a Bible in our own language today.

Context is very important when it comes to Bible study, and one of the best ways to get the context of a passage is to put the events of that passage into a timeline. Chronological Bibles, Bible timelines, and Gospel Harmonies are Bible study tools that will help you do that.

The chronological study method will allow you to break down and order complex Bible events into smaller parts. Following this method of study will increase your understanding of the Bible, and also help you to make connections that you might have otherwise missed. This method also includes genealogical studies, which can turn even boring Bible genealogies into an exciting Bible study!

Chapter 7 Discussion Questions

1. How did a limited understanding of the Scriptures among the *common people* lead to corruption within the church leadership?

2. The translators of the first English Bibles had to:
    A) Study to learn theology and different languages
    B) Be brave enough to hold to their convictions
    C) Stand alone against the powerful establishment
    D) All of the above

3. What motivated these men to translate the Bible into English? What helped them to prepare, to labor, and to take the stand they took, even as they risked their own lives?

4. The Reformers took a stand against an institutional church that had gone astray. How do institutions like a church lose their purpose? How can individuals within the institution avoid losing sight of their original goals?

5. God used a wicked man, King Henry VIII, to fund the first government-approved English Bible. Does God still use unsaved men to accomplish His purposes today? Why?

6. A chronological Bible rearranges the scriptures:
    A) In sequence
    B) In order of events
    C) By progression
    D) All of the above

7. A chronological Bible Study combines which two Bible Study methods?

Chapter 8

King James Only?
What To Do With the King James Bible

And these words which I command you today shall be in your heart. You shall teach them diligently to your children, and shall talk of them when you sit in your house, when you walk by the way, when you lie down, and when you rise up.
- Deuteronomy 6:6, 7

The King James Bible is the greatest achievement of English literature, more influential by far across the world than any comparable work. Yet today it has become a source of controversy. Within some circles of Christianity, the over 400 year-old King James Version (KJV) is regarded as archaic and lacking in relevance when compared to more modern translations. However, other believers insist on a "King James Only" ethic, rejecting all other modern translations as corruptions of the supposedly more pure King James Version.

The conflict between these two polar opposite sides over the King James translation has come to be known as the King James Controversy. As we shall see in this chapter, both positions are inherently foolish, and you shouldn't let either of them become a source of distraction as you study your Bible.

History of the King James Version

The long reign of Queen Elizabeth had brought a measure of stability to England, but political and religious conflicts still simmered just below the surface. When King James I ascended to the throne, he ruled over a divided kingdom. Papists (as Roman Catholics were called during that period of time) longed for England to return to the Roman Catholic Church, while the Protestants believed the Reformation in England had not gone nearly far enough.

Meanwhile, the King also had to take into account the influence of the clergy of the Anglican Church, who formed one of England's most powerful, privileged, and wealthy elite. There was also Parliament, which was always seeking to expand its power, among whose members the Puritans were heavily represented. Finally there were the extreme Protestants and Puritans called the Separatists, who wanted the government out of church affairs entirely. Some of these later travelled as Pilgrims to America.

In January of 1604 King James held a conference of religious leaders at the Hampton Court Palace to discuss matters such as church service, church ministers, church maintenance, and church discipline. This conference was largely a failure, but the effort was salvaged by Dr. John Reynolds of Oxford, who proposed a new English translation of the Bible. This idea was something the various factions of the conference could agree upon, so King James made the decision to endorse the project.

The Bishop's Bible, first printed in 1568, had been overcome by the much more popular Geneva Bible, which had won out due to its excellent scholarship, accuracy of translation, and its extensive commentary. However, the marginal notes were very controversial. For example, they proclaimed the Pope to be the Anti-Christ and questioned the divine right of Kings to rule over the people.

King James and the leaders of the Anglican Church agreed that a new translation was needed for the people, one that contained notes only for the purpose of scriptural cross-referencing and the clarification of certain Hebrew and Greek words. About four dozen learned men were assembled for this task. They were divided into six groups, two of which met at Cambridge, two at Oxford, and two at Westminster.

The first group of ten men at Westminster was assigned to the Old Testament from Genesis to 2 Kings, and the second group of seven scholars translated the Epistles. At Cambridge the first group, consisting of eight men, were assigned 1 Chronicles through Ecclesiastes, while the second group of seven men were assigned the Apocryphal books. Meanwhile at Oxford, the first group of seven men was assigned the prophetic books of Isaiah through Malachi, while the final group of eight scholars were given the four Gospels, Acts, and the Book of Revelation.

When producing this new translation, these scholars used the Tyndale New Testament, the Coverdale Bible, the Matthews Bible, the Great Bible, the Geneva Bible, and even the Roman Catholic Rheims New Testament as sources. From 1605 to 1606 these learned men engaged in private research, and from 1607 to 1609 the work was assembled. In 1610 the new Bible went to press. The finished work was revealed to the public in 1611, in the form of a huge folio edition. The full title page read:

"The | HOLY | Bible, | Conteyning the Old Testament, | AND THE NEW, | Newly Translated out of the Original | tongues: & with the former Translations | diligently compared and revised by his | Majesties special Comandement. | Appointed to be read in Churches | Imprinted at London by Robert | Barker, Printer to the Kings | most excellent Majestie | Anno Dom. 1611"

The New Testament was published in the same year, with the entire Bible published the following year in 1612. This translation came to be known as the Authorized Version, and was later called the King James Version after the King who had ordered the translation. By the end of 1612, large-sized Bibles were produced and chained to every church pulpit in England. After that, printing of normal-sized Bibles began so people could own their own personal copy of the new Bible.

The Authorized Version of the Anglican Church was not forced on the people, so it took a generation for it to surpass the more popular Geneva Bible. Today many Protestant churches embrace the King James Version as the only "legitimate" English translation, not realizing that it was never intended to be a Protestant translation at all! In fact, one of the main reasons it was published was to compete with the Geneva Bible, which was the one truly Protestant translation of that time.

However, the original 1611 King James did contain the Apocrypha, and the King threatened anyone who dared to print a Bible without the Apocrypha with heavy fines and a year in prison. Many advocates of the "King James Only" position would be horrified to learn these facts, but sadly most Protestants are almost completely ignorant of the history of their faith.

Advantages of the King James Version

Among the many advantages of the King James Version, the most obvious is its unequalled contribution to English language and literature. The style and dialect of the King James Bible is unique in that it was not written in the English language of the day, whether as written by scholars or as spoken in the conversation of the streets.

Instead, the combination of almost fifty learned men, translating from the original languages, combined with improvements made to already existing English translations, produced the most excellent and beautiful work of the English language that has ever been written. Even the renowned atheist Aldous Huxley said of the King James Version:

"...the great historical fact that, for three centuries, this book has been woven into the life of all that is best and noblest in English history; ...that it is written in the noblest and purest English, and abounds in exquisite beauties of mere literary form; and, finally, that it forbids the veriest hind who never left his village to be ignorant of the existence of other countries and other civilizations, and of a great

past, stretching back to the furthest limits of the oldest nations in the world." - Science and Education Essays, No. 15, The School Boards: What They Can Do, and What They May Do, Macmillan, London, 1893, pp. 396–402.

Many of the words and phrases from the King James have filtered down into our everyday language, and the 1611 version has influenced thousands of books, plays, and other works of literature. Phrases such as "by the skin of his teeth," "a house divided against itself cannot stand," "a drop in the bucket," "to everything there is a season," "don't cast your pearls before swine," "to the ends of the earth," "bite the dust," "a fly in the ointment," and dozens of other examples all have their origin in the King James Bible.

It took about 50 years for the King James to surpass the very popular Geneva Bible, and after that it had no rivals in the English-speaking world for over 200 years. The King James Bible turned out to be not only an excellent translation, but it became the most printed book in the history of the world, and the only book in existence with over one billion copies in print.

The King James Version is still widely used today, especially in foreign countries. Due to its worldwide distribution and the great length of time that it was the most popular translation, it still has widespread familiarity within the church. Furthermore, because it was the preeminent English translation for so long, most study materials, as mentioned in previous chapters, were written exclusively for this version up until just a generation ago.

Finally, the formal King James Version has some

special features that previous translations lacked. Along with an extensive cross-reference, there are explanatory notes on certain Greek and Hebrew words. Extra words that were added by the translators for clarity are marked in the text by italics so readers will know those words didn't appear in the original Hebrew or Greek.

Overall, the King James Version is one of the finest translations ever produced. Today it still continues to be highly influential and widely used.

Disadvantages of the KJV

There are also some downsides to the King James Version, the first being that it's over 400 years old. The English language itself has changed significantly since 1611, making the phrasing of the King James seem outdated and difficult to read. If you didn't grow up reading the King James, it's likely you find the poetic old English more frustrating than beautiful.

For example, when we read the word "hope" in the Bible we tend to think of its meaning today, as a synonym for "wish." However, in 1611 the word "hope" was a much stronger term which meant "to expect." See how that difference in the understanding of the word hope affects the reading of a verse like Hebrews 11:1:

Now faith is the substance of things (wished) for, the evidence of things not seen.

Or...

Now faith is the substance of things (expected), the evidence of things not seen.

Many similar examples could be cited. It's easy to see how the archaic 1611 English of the King James Version can present a hurdle for new Bible students. In fact, I've often thought about creating a King James-to-Modern English dictionary just to make it easier for King James readers!

Another problem with the King James Version is the lack of manuscripts that were available to the King James translators, especially with regard to the Old Testament. They had access to the *Samaritan Pentateuch,* a version of the Pentateuch used by the Samaritans with place names changed to match names in Samaria, and they had access to the Hebrew Masoretic text.

The oldest copy of the Hebrew Scriptures available to them was the *Aleppo Codex.* The word "codex" comes from the Latin and simply means an ancient book. The *Aleppo Codex* was produced around the year 950 A.D. in the city of Aleppo, but it was missing the Pentateuch (the first five books of the Bible). The only other manuscript they had was the *Leningrad Codex* which did contain the entire Old Testament, but was written about 60 years later in 1008 AD.

These two manuscripts together represented the Masoretic text, sometimes referred to as the Received Text, and it would be worthwhile to take a moment to describe exactly how the church "received" it. In the first century church there was no New Testament yet, as it was still in the process of being written. Most believers read from the Greek translation of the Old Testament called the *Septuagint*. This translation was produced in Alexandria, Egypt, about 100 years before Christ's birth.

Greek was the universal language of that time, much like English is today. There were a variety of Hebrew and Aramaic translations of the Old Testament available, but many Hellenized Jews, spread all across the Roman Empire in the diaspora, primarily spoke Greek, and some didn't know Hebrew at all. To accommodate these Greek-speaking Jews, the *Septuagint* was translated, taking its name because it was supposedly translated by 70 Hebrew scholars in 70 days' time.

We know Jesus used the Hebrew and Aramaic, as well as the *Septuagint* translations. In later years, as the church expanded further into the Greek-speaking world through Paul's missionary journeys and other efforts, the *Septuagint* became the favored translation of the gentile converts who were not able to read Hebrew. There were also some minor differences in translation which actually supported Christian doctrine, making the *Septuagint* even more popular among the early church.

The Jews of that time did not like this at all. They regarded Christianity as a heretical sect of Judaism, and hated the Christians who, from their point of view, had abandoned Jerusalem before the Romans destroyed it in 70 AD. They were especially upset that the Greek translation of their own Scriptures had been hijacked by these corrupted heretics, and that it was being used to spread the false beliefs of Christianity, in their view.

The destruction of Jerusalem had greatly reduced the number of Hebrew texts in circulation, so there was an urgency within the Jewish community to produce a "perfect text" in order to preserve the Hebrew Scriptures. A man named Rabbi Akiba headed this effort, producing what would later become known as the Masoretic text. Rabbi Akiba hated the Christians above all, and some of his followers attempted to claim that Akiba was actually the Messiah, and not Jesus Christ.

Rabbi Akiba's translation became preeminent when it was adopted by the Masoretes, a group of scribes and Hebrew scholars who operated between the 7th and 11th centuries, with schools in Tiberias and Jerusalem in Israel, and also in Babylonia. Their reputation and prestige arose from the accuracy and error-control of their copying techniques, resulting in their texts having an established authority in the Jewish community.

The *Aleppo Codex* and the *Leningrad Codex* were the oldest copies of the Masoretic text available to the King James translators. In fact, if you were a Bible translator living any time between 1611 and 1946, these two ancient books and the *Samaritan Pentateuch* were the only sources available to you. This all changed in 1947 with the discovery of the Dead Sea Scrolls at Qumran.

In the caves at Qumran, a library of scrolls was discovered, including some Hebrew and Aramaic texts, some that matched the *Septuagint,* and some that were unique. This not only provided a third source for the Old Testament Scriptures, but it also allowed for cross-referencing between the different versions, an effort that would hopefully lead to a final Old Testament translation that was more accurate overall. As of today, there are three major projects being carried out in different parts of the world by Bible scholars attempting to do just that.

However, the King James translators in the early 1600's, though they were brilliant scholars of exceptional character, were limited by the Hebrew sources available to them. For those Christians who strongly advocate a "King James Only" approach today, it is another irony that their beloved Old Testament "Received Text" was originally produced by a Rabbi who hated Jesus and who would have bitterly hated them.

This leads to the final drawback of the King James Version: the spiritual pride of the King James Only advocates and the needless strife, division, and controversy they have stirred up within the church. Yes, the King James is by far the most influential book in the history of the English speaking world, with a rich history and tradition within the church. Yes, there are certainly major problems with some of the more modern translations (we will look at those in the next two chapters).

Yet the King James Version, through no fault of its own, or its translators, also has its issues. It had limited manuscript sources to draw from, and when published it included the books of the Apocrypha. One wonders whether the "King James Only" zealots would also endorse the Roman Church's decision to add the Apocryphal books to the Bible at the Council of Trent?

The idea that believers who love God and desire to

be students of God's Word are somehow deficient because they refuse to use the King James Version as their primary translation for reading and study is absurd. For anyone to think he is spiritually superior, simply because he uses the King James while others do not, reeks of spiritual pride and borders on idolatry.

The truth of the matter is most King James Only advocates have never considered these points because they are ignorant of them, something to keep in mind if you ever encounter a person like this. With just the information you've read in this chapter, you know more than 95% of those Christians who hold the "King James Only" position.

Should You Use The King James Version?

The King James Version of 1611 is without a doubt one of the best Bible translations available. I criticize the "King James Only" position from the perspective of a person who absolutely loves the King James Bible. It is the Bible I grew up with, and even today when I hear Scripture quoted from other translations, translations that I know are both good and reliable, the words don't sound right to my ears.

I don't mind working around the old English terminology, as it seems a small price to pay to enjoy the beautiful language of this Bible. I do make use of many other translations in my studies, but the King James has been programmed into me since the time I was a small boy. It's how I learned God's Word, so to me it is the basis of my relationship with Him. I love the King James Version and I always will.

But what if you don't share my experience and history with the King James Bible? Here is my recommendation for study purposes: You should use both the King James and a modern translation that works for you. For devotional reading, use your preferred modern translation. Devotional reading is supposed to be enjoyable, and it will be hard to enjoy your devotional reading if you have to plod your way through unfamiliar language and phrasing.

However, when engaging in in-depth Bible study, you should use the King James plus your modern translation. This is not just to help you understand the older English of the King James. You will find there are other substantial benefits to Bible study when you use both versions together.

There are some things the modern translations miss which the King James Version, in its thoroughness and exactness of translation, does not. This is also true in the other direction, where a modern translation will improve upon the King James translation, although that doesn't happen as often. Remember, the issue isn't the inspiration or accuracy of God's Word, but rather the quality of the translations we have access to. If you are comparing the two versions side by side, it will be easier for you to identify those portions of Scripture where one translation is better than the other.

Another benefit to your study will be an increased familiarity with the King James. Even today, phrases from the King James appear often in secular literature and drama, and knowing that version better will help you recognize them and gain a deeper appreciation for your culture.

Beyond that, many Bible study resources are based on the King James, especially older books and materials. Often you'll find older books on the Bible to be more weighty and substantive, especially when compared to many modern Christian publications, and knowing the language of the King James will help you get more out of these study materials.

Therefore, my recommendation is that you conduct your Bible study with both the King James Version and a second quality modern translation of your choice. Your Bible study will benefit immensely from this dual approach. Of course, this leads immediately to the question, "Which modern translation should I choose?" We will examine that question in the next two chapters.

Bible Study Tool #8
Historical And Cultural Bible Commentaries

One of the keys to understanding the Bible is being able to place things within their proper context. Basic word studies aren't very useful if you don't understand the verse within which that word was used. With verse studies, you need the context of the verses both before and after the verse you're looking at. Placing the passage in its literary context also makes a difference, because history and poetry are two different types of literature, and you don't read them in the same way.

Two more contexts that are very important are the

historical and cultural contexts of a passage. The Biblical writers wrote for their intended audience, not for 21st century Americans. As a result, much of the backdrop in their stories is implied, and not directly explained. This is especially true when it comes to history and culture. The Bible study tools to help you avoid these problems are historical and cultural commentaries.

Consider this example of historical context: When Mark wrote his Gospel, he didn't go into great detail about how Rome was in control of Judea at the time. Everyone who Mark knew already understood that Judea was firmly under the dominion of the Roman Empire, and all of his readers knew it, so there was no need for him to explain it in any detail. Yet when reading the Gospel of Mark today, if you didn't realize that Judea was actually ruled by Rome, then some key events from the story might not make any sense to you.

Cultural context is equally important when it comes to interpreting the Bible. Consider this passage, where Jesus is rebuking the Pharisees for their religious hypocrisy:

He said to them, "All too well you reject the commandment of God, that you may keep your tradition. For Moses said, 'Honor your father and your mother'; and, 'He who curses father or mother, let him be put to death.' But you say, 'If a man says to his father or mother, "Whatever profit you might have received from me is Corban"—' (that is, a gift to God), then you no longer let him do anything for his father or his mother, making the word of God of no effect

through your tradition which you have handed down. And many such things you do."
– Mark 7:9-13 (NKJ)

What is Jesus talking about in verse 11: "But you say, 'If a man says to his father or mother, *"Whatever profit you might have received from me is Corban"*—' *(that is, a gift to God)"*? If you were able to consult a book on New Testament culture, you would find that the Pharisees could declare a portion of their money to be "Corban," which meant it was set aside for the Lord's use. Dedicating some of your money exclusively for the Lord's use is a good thing to do, so what was the problem?

Jesus was calling them out publicly for breaking the commandment to honor their father and mother. Instead of spending some of their money to care for their elderly parents as they should have been doing, they declared that money to be Corban. Since it was now set aside for God, so they claimed, they wouldn't be able to use it to care for their parents, thus twisting the Law of Moses to suit their own purposes. None of this would be comprehensible to a modern reader who didn't have access to these cultural insights.

When you think about it, you realize history and culture touch upon almost everything that a society does and affects almost every way people behave. Things like language, clothing, shelter, work, religion, education, values, arts, government, recreational activities, beliefs, shared ideas, family, food, tools, and customs are all affected by history and culture.

The task of interpreting the Bible, which was written by and to people living in very different cultural contexts from our contemporary Western society, at times can seem monumental. Yet, it's also easy to see how improving your understanding of the historical and cultural background of the Bible's stories can be a huge benefit to you in your progress as a student of the Bible.

The opposite is also true. A Bible student can easily forget that studying the Bible is a lot like a cross-cultural encounter, and instead read her own modern cultural assumptions into the biblical text. With a solid understanding of the cultural factors involved, we won't make the mistake of expecting 1st century characters to react in the same way as 21st century people who have access to modern technologies and ideas.

How would a Bible student make use of cultural and historical commentaries? Historical and cultural studies are actually studies about the Bible, rather than studies of the Bible itself. The goal of these studies is to learn how people thought, communicated, and lived in the ancient world during the Old Testament and the New Testament, and even in the Intertestamental period in between. This is accomplished through the study of key people and groups, as well as the literary, cultural, theological, and political events that form the background to the Bible.

The result of cultural and historical Bible studies is greater insight into the Scriptures, informed by the sociology, philosophy, politics, literature, geography, and history of the Ancient Near East for the Old Testament, and the Greco-Roman world for the New Testament. This allows the Bible student to interpret Scripture in light of the history and culture of the people to whom the book was originally addressed.

The use of cultural and historical studies has the potential to greatly enrich our understanding of the Bible and lead us into a deeper understanding of who God is and how He expects us to live. There are four major advantages of cultural and historical studies:

First, studying the history of the ancient world helps us to learn about the events that shaped the lives of people in the ancient world. For example, we read in the opening verses of Luke chapter two:

1 And it came to pass in those days, that there went out a decree from Caesar Augustus that all the world should be taxed.
2 (And this taxing was first made when Cyrenius was governor of Syria.) – Luke 2:1-2 (KJV)

From these verses you might do a study about Caesar Augustus, or Cyrenius' governorship of Syria. Studies of this kind, while not a requirement for your Christian faith, can often help to reinforce it by making links between recorded history and the Bible.

Second, learning about the languages of the ancient world is a method we can use to gain insight into the semantics, idioms, and metaphors used in Hebrew, Aramaic, and Greek. For example, consider Psalm 10:15:

Break the arm of the wicked and evildoer; call

his wickedness to account till you find none.
- Psalm 10:15

In this verse, the psalmist isn't asking God to literally break the physical arm of each of his enemies. "Break the arm" is a Hebrew idiom that means "to break the power of." Sometimes a literal English translation of a Greek or Hebrew idiom or metaphor comes across as strange to our English ears, so a cultural and historic study of the phrase can help us to better understand the meaning of the verse.

Third, the study of the archaeology of the Greco-Roman world helps us to learn about the lifestyle and material culture of the people who lived in that world. Sometimes we have to stop and remind ourselves that even though people haven't really changed over the centuries, their lifestyle has changed radically. We know there was no Internet or cell phones in the ancient world, for example, but learning about what things they did have can help us understand them better, and thereby help us to better understand the Bible.

Lastly, studying the literature of the Ancient Near East (ANE) and the Greco-Roman world helps us to relate to the heart and soul of the people who lived in the world which Israel and the early church inhabited. Comparing other ANE texts to the Old Testament shows us that the Biblical authors were aware of and influenced by the writings of the nations that surrounded them. Knowing this can improve our understanding of the corresponding writings in the Bible. Likewise, the literature of the first century gives us context for the writings of the New Testament, the most obvious being when Paul quotes secular authors in his ministry (Acts 17:28; Titus 1:12).

A note to Pastors and Bible teachers: If you have invested the time and energy to perform historical and cultural studies, obviously you will want to share the discoveries you've made in your teaching and preaching, and you should do so. However, take care that you are always edifying the people rather than discouraging them. Use historical and cultural study tools to enhance your people's understanding of the biblical text, increasing their confidence in God's Word instead of undermining it.

When the congregation only hears a steady stream of "where this Bible translation gets it wrong is..." or "what the Greek really says here," they're being taught that they shouldn't trust their own ability to read the Bible. Think about it: Why would an average believer ever read the Bible on his own when he is constantly told he has no hope of understanding it because he doesn't know the original languages?

Cultural and historical studies can give us a much deeper understanding of the background of the Bible. However, many cultural and historical Bible study resources are written by scholars who are not even believing Christians, so you do have to be somewhat careful with these materials. Take the time and make the effort to determine where a particular Bible scholar is coming from, and don't rely on this type of study exclusively.

For example, sometimes information from cultural and historical studies is used to claim that a biblical text doesn't mean what it clearly seems to say. Therefore, you should use cultural and historical studies as an enhancement of your Bible study, but not as the foundation of it. I certainly believe background studies can shed important light on a text, but I'm also convinced that God has given us His Word in such a way that believers can reach a good understanding of the text without any advanced training in the Bible's cultural and historical background.

Historical commentaries are typically laid out in the historical order of the events they cover, as you would expect. However, in cultural commentaries the entries are usually arranged topically. A good example of a historical Bible commentary is the *IVP Bible Background Commentary for the Old and New Testaments*. Examples of cultural commentaries include *A Cultural Handbook to the Bible* and *The New Testament in Antiquity: A Survey of the New Testament within Its Cultural Context.*

Bible Study Method #8
Book Background Study

The goal of the book survey study is to gain a better understanding of the background of a particular book of the Bible so that you study that book more effectively. Here are the steps to a Bible book background study:

1. Choose a book of the Bible to study

For beginners it's a good idea to pick a shorter book, but it should also be a book you have a greater interest in, because that will help to motivate you through the study.

2. Assemble your reference tools

You should have a Bible handbook, a Bible Atlas, Bible commentaries for that book, and a Bible dictionary or Bible encyclopedia. Bible students will usually prefer some reference tools over others, so keep track of which reference tools you use and make a note of the ones that are the most helpful so you can return to them in future studies.

3. Attempt to discover the following:

- Who is the author of the book?
- Where was the author when the book was written?
- What was the geographical setting of the book?
- Who was the original intended audience of the book?
- What is the date of the book?
- What historical events occurred just prior to the time the book was being written?
- What historical events occurred during the time the book was written?
- What historical events occurred immediately after the book was written?
- What future events or persons are anticipated in the book?
- What was the reigning culture of the day?
- What was the current political situation?
- Why do you think the author wrote the book?
- How does the book fit into the overall arc of the Bible story?

4. Summarize Your Research

At this point you should have a rough idea what the

book is about. Organize your notes on index cards or in an outline in a way that's most useful to you.

5. Create a personal goal for further study

Write down your personal goal for further study of that book. At this point it's likely you've come across something about the book that's piqued your curiosity enough to interest you to find out more. It might be one of the themes covered in the book, or maybe a certain Bible character, or any number of possibilities. As you study this Bible book more using the Bible study methods in the chapters that follow, you'll learn many different things along the way, but make a note of one specific thing you're going to be focusing on.

Summary

The King James Version is one of the greatest translations of the Bible and the most influential literary work of the English language ever created. Though over 400 years old, it still exerts a strong influence on the church today. While it is not perfect, it is superior to many modern translations, and is improved upon by some of the better modern translations.

When one considers the facts that the King James as originally published contained the Apocrypha and was designed to be a direct competitor to the Protestant's Geneva Bible, and that its Old Testament is based on the Masoretic text which was originally produced as an explicitly anti-Christian Hebrew translation, the position of the "King James Only" advocates makes very little sense.

At the same time, it would be a mistake to discount the worth of the King James Version simply because it is old and its language is out of date. You should own a King James Bible and study it in tandem with the modern translation that you prefer.

Just as it is important to learn the history and background of how we got our Bible, it's also very important for us to understand the history and background of the ancient world in which the Bible was written. Historical and cultural commentaries can give us insight into the world in which the Bible's characters lived.

Learning about the history, figures of speech, archaeology, and literature of the ancient world gives us a better context for the writings of the Bible, and this knowledge can lead us into a deeper understanding of God's Word and of God Himself. We don't want to place too much emphasis on historical and cultural studies, but at the same time they can be very helpful.

In the next chapter we'll look at other Bible versions beyond the King James Version. This will give you the information you need to choose the best modern Bible translation for yourself. We'll also examine yet another Bible study tool, and show you another Bible study method: the Book Survey Study.

Chapter 8 Discussion Questions

1. Prior to reading this chapter, what was your impression of the King James Version?

2. While the Bishop's Bible received the endorsement of Queen Elizabeth and the Anglican Church, the Geneva Bible was much more popular with the people, largely due to its:
    A) Excellency of scholarship
    B) Accuracy of translation
    C) Extensive commentary notes in the margins
    D) All of the above

3. King James wanted a new translation to unify the people. Why was it important for the church to have one common text at that time? Why is that not as important today?

4. The Bible says, *"Every matter must be established by the testimony of two or three witnesses"* (2 Corinthians 13:1). How was this principle applied when the King James was translated? How many scholars were used? How many source texts were used? How did this help insure the translation's accuracy?

5. How do historical and cultural commentaries like the *IVP Bible Background Commentary for the Old and New Testaments* help provide modern day application to The Holy Bible?

9. What is the purpose of the Book Background study method?

10. How does doing a Book Background study help you to select a good goal for further study later?

Chapter 9

Lost In Translations
Modern Versions of the English Bible

The Jews proved more generous-minded than those in Thessalonica, for they accepted the message most eagerly and studied the Scriptures every day to see if what they were now being told were true.
- Acts 17:11 (PHL)

As recently as fifty years ago the King James, or Authorized Version, of the Bible was considered by many to be the only reliable translation. Choosing a Bible involved selecting the color and deciding if you wanted leather binding or not. Today, dozens of English translations are available. How does one decide which is best?

First, we need to recognize that there is no single translation that is the "best." Even the New Testament writers themselves quote from several Greek translations of the Old Testament. Today we have no perfect translation, but some are better than others, and there are a number which are excellent.

The real question is this: Which version is best for your particular needs? In this chapter we'll look at some of the major alternatives to the KJV and where they came from. This information will be helpful to you when it comes to choosing which modern translation you will use as your main resource for personal Bible study.

Other Bible Translations

The King James Version was the Bible of choice for the English-speaking world for over 200 years, both in England and in America. In 1833, after Noah Webster finished his famous dictionary, he produced his own English Bible. However, the King James was still very popular, so Webster's version never really took off.

It wasn't until the 1880's that the first serious challenger to the King James arose: the Revised Standard Version (RSV). This was the Church of England's own planned replacement for the King James, and it was the first modern translation to gain widespread acceptance. It was also the first modern Bible translation that did not include the Apocryphal books.

As late as the 1880's every Bible, both Protestant and Catholic, contained the Apocrypha. These included many printings of the Tyndale-Matthews Bible, the Great Bible, the Bishop's Bible, the Protestant Geneva Bible, and the King James Version.

Such was the influence of the Roman Catholic Church that it took 335 years to undo their decision to add these books which should never have been included in the Bible to begin with.

American Standard Version

America responded to the new English translation in 1901 by producing the American Standard Version (ASV), a nearly identical version of the Revised Standard Version (RSV). The ASV was also widely embraced in churches across America, and for many decades it was the leading non-British modern translation of the Bible.

In 1971 it was revised again and published as the New American Standard Version (NAS or NASV). The NAS is considered to be the most accurate, word-for-word translation of the Greek and Hebrew Scriptures into modern English that has ever been produced.

The NAS is still one of the most popular versions among theologians, professors, scholars, and seminary students today because of its focus on accuracy. However, some readers have difficulty with it because it is such a direct and literal translation, resulting in English phrasing that sounds wooden and doesn't flow easily when read aloud. Another update was published in 1995 which seeks to use more modern English while preserving the literal nature of the translation.

Williams New Testament

Charles Bray Williams was a student of Greek and Latin and a college educator. He spent twenty years perfecting his translation, which was released in 1937 as the Williams New Testament (WIL). His aim was to translate the Greek New Testament into a readable and more understandable English in "the language of the people."

It is not a word-for-word translation like an interlinear Bible. Instead, it is a translation of the thoughts of the writers with a faithful reproduction of their diction and style.

Worrel New Testament

A. S. Worrell, spent two and one-half years devoted to the Worrel New Testament (WOR), which was released in 1907. In Worrell's words, "It was done with the view of pleasing the Supreme Critic, at Whose judgment bar he will have to account for the manner in which he has handled His word." The Greek text of Westcott and Hort was used in the preparation of this work, making it one of the more accurate of the early modern translations.

Amplified Bible

The Amplified Bible (AMP) was first published in 1958. It is the fruit of tens of thousands of hours of research by Dr. Frances Siewert. Beginning with the very literal ASV, she added additional words in brackets that help provide a better understanding of the meaning of the original language. These additional bracketed words make the AMP somewhat difficult to read, but it has nonetheless become a very popular "second Bible" for serious Bible students.

New Testament in Modern English

Also called the Phillips Translation, the New Testament in Modern English (PHL) was completed by Bible scholar J. B. Phillips in 1958. Phillips had a special knack of rendering difficult and long sentences into very understandable English. He even translates well some of

178

the Greek puns and word plays that usually are lost. It can be very helpful to have a copy of Phillips nearby, especially when studying the epistles of Paul.

New American Bible

A Roman Catholic translation, the New American Bible (NAB) was the work of the Confraternity of Christian Doctrine, and was first published in 1970. It is the version used in the American Catholic lectionary. In 2011 a Revised Edition was published. The NAB is a more literal translation, especially the 1986 revision of the New Testament.

Good News Bible

The Good News Bible, also known as Today's English Version (TEV), was translated by Robert G. Bratcher with six other scholars, and was completed in 1976. This very free, though very accurate, translation avoids the use of traditional biblical vocabulary. This makes the TEV somewhat unpopular among traditional Christian groups, yet it communicates especially well with youth and the unchurched.

New International Version

Due to the difficulty many readers had with the NAS, in 1973 the New International Version (NIV) was produced, and completed in 1978. The 115 evangelical scholars who collaborated on the NIV offered a new method of Bible translation called "dynamic equivalence." Dynamic equivalence was designed as a "phrase-for-phrase" method of translation, as opposed to the more accurate "word-for-word" translation of the NAS.

This new modern translation was created for ease of reading down to the sixth grade level, and was intended to appeal to a larger and possibly less educated audience. It combines contemporary, literary English with traditional biblical vocabulary.

However, the NIV left out many Bible verses and portions of verses, including verses about the Blood of Jesus, which led critics to jokingly refer to it as the "Nearly Inspired Version." Despite these serious deficiencies, the NIV was the best-selling modern English translation of the Bible for the remainder of the 20th century.

A major revision of the NIV was released in early 2011. While it changed only about 5% of the text from the previous edition (1984), the changes are significant, and it almost reads like a new translation. This new revision also includes "gender-neutral" language when referring to people, similar to the NRSV (see below).

New King James Version

In 1982, Thomas Nelson Publishers produced what they called the New King James Version (NKJ or NKJV). Their intention was to keep the basic wording of the King James the same in order to appeal to King James Version loyalists, while changing only the most obscure old English words and the Elizabethan "thee, thy, thou" pronouns.

This plan generated considerable interest, but when the publishers discovered the changes they were making weren't enough to allow them to legally copyright the result, they had to make more significant revisions, an action which ultimately defeated their stated purpose. The NKJ was never taken seriously by Bible scholars, but it is a decent enough translation and has enjoyed a degree of public acceptance, simply because of its clever "New King James Version" marketing name.

New Jerusalem Bible

The New Jerusalem Bible (NJB) was published in 1985 to revise and update the text and notes of the Jerusalem Bible (JB) of 1966. That version, based on a French translation, was an elegant, literary rendering of the Bible, perhaps the most poetic since the KJV. Both the JB and NJB were projects of Roman Catholic scholars, and the notes reflect a modern and more liberal perspective. As with the NAB (and all Roman Catholic Bibles), the Apocryphal books are still included.

New Revised Standard Version

The New Revised Standard Version (NRSV) was published in 1989 by the National Council of Churches. It was intended to update the Revised Standard Version. While following the literal tradition of the RSV, the NRSV eliminates much of the archaic language. Another element distinctive to the NRSV is the use of gender inclusive pronouns to replace male pronouns when the original writers meant both men and women. However, the NRSV does not change masculine pronouns referring to God.

Revised English Bible

The Revised English Bible (REB), also completed in

1989, is a thorough revision of the New English Bible. Like the original, it was translated by a committee of British scholars, representing all the major Christian traditions in the United Kingdom. Many readers find it to be an excellent translation for personal reading and study, though its British idioms make it less popular in the United States.

Contemporary English Version

The Contemporary English Version (CEV) was a completely new translation published by the American Bible Society in 1995. Originally intended as a children's translation, it uses a very simple, contemporary style. It is independent of traditional translations and freer of traditional "biblical" terms, making it an especially good translation for people who speak English as a second language.

New Living Translation

Published in 1996, the New Living Translation (NLT) is the product of 90 Bible scholars from around the world, from various theological backgrounds and denominations. This is a very readable translation, while remaining more faithful to the original texts than the Living Bible paraphrase it was designed to replace. An updated version was published in 2004.

English Standard Version

In 2001, a major Bible translation project was launched, with the goal of bridging the gap between the simple readability of the NIV and the extremely precise accuracy of the NAS. The result was the English Standard

Version (ESV). Developed by a translation team of more than 100 scholars, the ESV has become quite popular. It is more readable than other literal translations, yet it is also a very accurate translation.

Holman Christian Standard Bible

The Holman Christian Standard Bible (HCSB) is also the product of nearly 100 scholars. The HCSB is another new word-for-word translation that strives to be both literally accurate and highly readable. It is not as literal as the ESV or NAS, but it is more literal than the NIV, making it a very popular translation.

Now It's Your Turn To Choose

As students of the Word of God, we need to make intelligent and informed decisions about which Bible translations we choose to read. On the liberal extreme, we find heretical new translations that attempt to change God's Word in order to make it politically correct. One example of this is Today's New International Version (TNIV), which seeks to remove all gender-specific references in the Bible, including references to God Himself! Not all modern translations are reliable, and some are very bad.

On the other hand, we don't want to overreact to a handful of poor modern translations by rejecting all new translations. We can't go to the other extreme of blindly rejecting any modern translation based on the idolatrous loyalty of some to the King James Version. We must always remember that the Protestant Reformation's main purpose was to liberate the Bible from the chains of ancient languages and bring it into that day's conversational language, which the best modern translations do very well.

Now that we've analyzed the various major Bible versions that are available to us, in the next chapter we will find which modern translation is the best one for you. In doing so, we both celebrate and reaffirm the glorious heritage that belongs to us today – a quality Bible translation in our own English language – thanks to the brave efforts of men of God going all the way back to William Tyndale, who fought and died that we might be able to have this.

One day Tyndale met a bureaucrat who criticized his efforts to translate the Bible into the commonly spoken English of his day. Tyndale boldly replied to the man, "If God spare my life, I will see to it that the boy who drives the plowshare knows more of the Scripture than you, Sir!"

Bible Study Tool #9
Bible Atlases

Bible atlases are manuals of Biblical geography, designed to benefit teachers and students of the Bible. They can contain various maps, as well as charts, diagrams, and sometimes even building plans. They accurately illustrate where cities and other principal locations throughout Bible history can be found.

Using maps is a valuable tool for Bible Study. Think about the maps used today. Road maps give insight into the distance between locations, which roads to take, and what points of interest to look for when traveling. Physical maps reveal the physical features of an area, such as the location of rivers, mountains, lakes, and seas.

Topographical maps use contour lines where each line represents the same elevation. This reveals the topography of the terrain, or the lay of the land. It's much more informative to see a topographical map than a flat map with no contours and curves. All of these play a critical role in our ability to accurately understand biblical events.

For example, there was a major highway that ran the full length of Israel. This trade route was of great importance, and it was the main reason Israel had so much interaction with the surrounding nations. Sites like Jerusalem and Megiddo had significant military advantages due to their topography, thus many battles took place there. Physical barriers such as rivers, seas, and lakes all played a major role in shaping biblical events. Understanding their significance gives us a greater understanding of the biblical narrative than we would otherwise have.

However, even a study Bible that includes a good set of maps isn't really sufficient, because they provide only a very wide-angle view of Bible lands. It would be like trying to understand the book of Ezekiel only by reading your study Bible's introduction to Ezekiel. To get all the benefits that Bible maps can give, you need to go far beyond the "Book of Maps" at the end of your Bible. You need to take the next step and get a Bible atlas.

The first Bible atlas, called the *Onomasticon* (meaning "a collection of names"), was written by Eusebius, the Bishop of Caesarea, in 325 A.D. Eusebius understood the value of geography to biblical studies, and his book contained a systematized index and encyclopedia of Bible sites and locations. Eusebius wanted his atlas to benefit Bible students who might never have the opportunity to visit Israel themselves. Eusebius' Onomasticon inspired many of the early pilgrimages to the Holy Land. Without his volume, we would not know the location of many biblical sites today.

Good atlases contain more than just maps. They illustrate the importance of geography as it relates to topography, history, archaeology, and climate. Today, with modern satellite imagery, Bible atlases are more useful than ever. Some excellent atlases for new Bible students are the *Macmillan Bible Atlas*, the *Rose Book of Bible Charts, Maps, and Time Lines*, and the *Zondervan Essential Atlas of the Bible*.

Bible Study Method #9
Book Survey Study

The purpose of the book survey study is to obtain a detailed overview of a particular book of the Bible. When used together with the Bible study methods described in the following chapters (the Chapter Study and the Book Synthesis Study), it will give the Bible student a comprehensive view of each book of the Bible.

The main goal of the book survey method is to gain a detailed understanding as to why the book was written, its context, its theme, its structure, and its content.

Step 1 - Read the book following these steps:

Read the whole book through in one sitting

The two longest books of the Bible are Psalms and Isaiah, and the average reader can get through those in just a few hours. Reading the book straight through in one sitting gives you a good overview of its contents.

The larger books can be divided into two sections if necessary, so you can read them with a break in between, but you should still read it all the way through as fast as possible.

Read the book in a modern translation

You will want to read the book in a translation where the language is current so it won't distract you from the content of the book.

Read the book as though the chapter and verse divisions weren't there

Read the book like you would any regular book, ignoring the chapter and verse reference numbers. This will give you a better feel for the flow of the book and the relationship of its various ideas to one another.

Read through the book three times

You will be surprised at what you notice in your second and third readings that you missed the first time through.

187

Read without referring to external notes

Concentrate on the text of the book itself without using any commentaries or study notes at this point.

Read through the book prayerfully

Ask God to speak to you by His Holy Spirit as you read, and pray that He opens your eyes to the lessons He wants you to learn.

Step 2 - Make notes on what you read

Take notes as you read, and write down your observations about what you're reading, especially during the second and third times through. Write down your impressions of the book and any important details that you uncover. Use these questions to help you:

What genre is the book?

Is the book law, historic, poetic, prophetic, biographic, correspondence, or narrative?

What do you think was the author's purpose?

Make note of your first impressions as you read.

What words does the author use most often?

What words does the author seem to consider to be important or significant?

Is there a key verse or a key statement?

For example, is there a verse like Revelation 1:19 that summarizes the entire Book of Revelation?

What is the literary style of the author?

How does the writing style relate to the book's message?

Does the author reveal his emotions in the writing?

How would the original readers have responded to this emotion? How do you respond to this emotion?

What do you believe the main theme is?

Make note of the main theme (or themes) of the book. Does the book have a major thrust or overall idea?

How is the book organized?

What are the organic divisions of the book? What influenced those natural divisions in the book (people, geography, historical events, culture)?

Remember that the chapters and verses (and in some translations, even paragraphs) were all added centuries after the original authors completed their work, so don't let those influence your answer to this question. Instead, look for divisions that emerge naturally from the book.

What people are central to the book?

Are there specific characters that are important? If so what part do they play in this book?

Step 3 - Do a background study of the book

If you have already done a Book Background study of that Bible book (as described in chapter 8), that will already contain useful information you can refer to for this study. If not, go ahead and do a Book Background study of the book now.

Step 4 - Make a horizontal chart of the book's contents

A horizontal chart is a visual representation of the book on one or more sheets of paper. It allows you to grasp the general details of the book as you draw them out pictorially. Follow these steps to create your horizontal chart:

Draw out the chapters

On a single sheet of paper, or more if needed, make as many vertical columns as there are chapters in the book you are studying.

Read through the book a fourth time

As you read through the book again you should start

noticing some major divisions. These will often match the chapter divisions, but not always. Write out headings for each of your major divisions using as few words as possible.

Read through the book a fifth time

As you do this, think of a short title for each chapter and record them just below the divisions you made in the previous step, placing each at the top of your columns. Good chapter titles are short, usually just one to four words. They should be picturesque, helping you to visualize the chapter contents, but they should also be taken from the text if possible. Each chapter title should be unique, and not repeated from chapter titles in other book studies.

Read through the book a sixth time

This time through the book you will create a series of titles for the paragraphs within each chapter. If you're reading a version that uses only Bible verses without paragraphs, divide the chapter into paragraph divisions that seem most logical to you. Most every modern translation will already be divided into paragraphs, however.

Step 5 - Create a basic outline of the book

Drawing from all the work you've done so far, create a preliminary outline of the book. You will use this again later in chapter 11 when you learn about the Book Synthesis Study in which you will make a more detailed outline of the book. Here are some helpful points:

Start your outline

List the major points of the book and organize them into an outline.

Organize your outline

Put the major points of your outline in sequence of descending importance. List the major points first followed by the minor points.

Refer to your notes

The chapter and paragraph titles you created will be helpful with your outline since they are usually grouped around the major ideas.

Check your outline

Refer to your Bible reference materials to compare your outline to those made by others. You can also compare your outline with that of another Bible student if you are studying together. See where your outlines differ and where they are similar. Remember there is no right or wrong answer. You may like your outline better than one made by an established Bible scholar, and that's perfectly fine.

Step 6 – Create a goal for personal study

This is the same as step 5 in the Book Background Study. At this point you may have already reached the goal you set there, or you may be closer to it than you were. If you have met your personal goal, then create a new one based on the work you've put in so far. If you're still working toward the goal you set in the previous study, you might want to adjust it slightly based on some of the new things you've learned.

Summary

There are a variety of modern Bible translations, many of which are excellent and a handful which are not very good at all. By understanding some basic information about the various Bible versions available today, you can make a more informed decision when the time comes to select which modern translation you will use.

We need to be careful not to throw the baby out with the bathwater by allowing the deficiencies of some modern translations to scare us away from all of them. At the same time, while we can deeply appreciate the marvel of the King James Version, we cannot worship it as an idol the way that some in the church have done.

Another Bible study tool that has become more beneficial with the advent of modern technology is the Bible atlas. With its maps, charts, and diagrams, a good atlas can bring the Bible to life and help Bible students who have never visited the Holy Land to gain a better idea of what it would be like to experience living there.

Gaining a better understanding of Bible geography will also help you perform more meaningful cultural and historical Bible studies and will be of equal benefit when analyzing the context of a Bible passage for expository studies.

Performing a Book Survey study will give you a detailed overview of one book of the Bible. It differs from the Book Background study described in chapter 8, because you will not use any external resources such as Bible commentaries until the very end of your survey.

When your Book Survey study is completed, you will have a good understanding of why the book was written, its context, its theme, its structure, and its content.

At this point we are definitely in the deep waters of Bible study. The concentrated information you've been exposed to in the last few chapters may have seemed overwhelming at times, but with God's help you have the ability to not only keep up, but to become a highly skilled Bible student through the use of these methods.

In the next chapter we'll finally answer the question, "Which Bible translation should I use?" We'll also take a look at Bible study software and online resources, and you will learn how to do a much more detailed study of an entire chapter of the Bible.

Chapter 9 Discussion Questions

1. Do you have a favorite version of the Bible? If so, what makes that one your favorite?

2. The Revised Standard Version (RSV) was the first Bible translation that did not include:
   A) Paul's letters to the gentile churches
   B) The Apocrypha
   C) References to the blood of Christ
   D) Chapter & verse numbering

3. It took over 50 years, or a little over a generation, for the King James Bible to gain widespread popularity and support. With so many versions available today, will there ever be another "universally accepted" translation like the KJV?

4. Consider what was happening in the 1880's, a period of American history known as the Gilded Age, or the Second Industrial Revolution: Scientists like Edison, Bell and Tesla were experimenting with electricity. Clara Barton established the Red Cross. New products like Coca-Cola were being invented and marketed. Do you think this drive for the "new" and "modern" was reflected in the church's desire for a new Bible to replace the King James Version?

5. What are some of the benefits and drawbacks of having so many different Bible versions available to us today?

6. What is the purpose or goal of a Book Survey study?

7. Which is the more challenging Bible study, the Book Background study or the Book Survey study? Why?

Chapter 10

Drawing Your Sword
Selecting the Right Bible for You

For the word of God is quick, and powerful, and sharper than any two-edged sword, piercing even to the dividing asunder of soul and spirit, and of the joints and marrow, and is a discerner of the thoughts and intents of the heart.
  - Hebrews 4:12 (KJV)

The Bible was originally written in Hebrew (Old Testament) and Greek (New Testament), so unless you happen to speak those languages, you will have to choose an English translation that you are comfortable using.

Choosing the Right Bible

There are three main types of Bible translations that you can choose from:
  1) Formal Equivalence
  2) Dynamic Equivalence
  3) Paraphrases

Don't let these heavy theological terms scare you off because I'm going to explain everything to you!

Formal Equivalence Translations

Formal equivalence emphasizes faithfulness to the original text by attempting a formal word-for-word translation, while paying close attention to the grammatical structure of the original language. The major advantage of formal equivalence translations is that they are more accurate, and thus better suited for serious Bible study.

However, there are also some disadvantages to formal equivalence translations. Idioms from the original languages that are translated literally into English can be difficult to understand. Also, since it is a word-for-word translation, the text doesn't always flow so easily, and readability suffers.

Formal Equivalence Translations:

King James Version
Young's Literal Translation
American Standard Version
Revised Standard Version
New King James Version
New Revised Standard Version
New American Standard Bible
English Standard Version
Lexham English Bible
New World Translation

My favorite formal translations are the King James Version and the English Standard Version, but all of them are excellent.

Dynamic Equivalence Translations

With dynamic equivalence, the translators try to bring out the meaning of the text in an easier to read format. Instead of translating word-for-word, these types of translations are more thought-for-thought.

The translators will look at each section of the text and reword it so that in their estimation it will better convey the meaning of the original writer.

One of the problems with the Dynamic Equivalent approach is that it's less accurate because it's not a true word-for-word translation, making it less reliable for in-depth Bible study.

It's also possible for the theological biases of the translators to impact the text. So for studying purposes always try to compare a dynamic equivalence translation to a formal translation when you can.

There are 2 sub-categories of Dynamic Equivalence translations: Intermediate and Functional Equivalence. If you envision a sliding scale with Formal Equivalence on one end, and Paraphrases (described in the next section) on the other end, Intermediate Equivalence translations would be closer to the Formal side while Functional Equivalence translations would be closer to the Paraphrases.

This means that Intermediate versions are closer to the original text, while Functional versions are freer translations that are more meaning-for-meaning than word-for-word.

Intermediate Dynamic Equivalence Translations:

New International Version
Today's New International Version
Holman Christian Standard Bible
Jerusalem Bible
New American Bible
New English Translation
Modern Language Bible

Functional Dynamic Equivalence translations:

New Jerusalem Bible
New English Bible
Revised English Bible
Good News Bible
Complete Jewish Bible
New Living Translation
New Century Version
God's Word Translation
Contemporary English Version

There are many very good dynamic equivalence translations, but I personally prefer the Holman Christian Standard Bible and the New Living Translation.

Paraphrases

A paraphrase is not really a true translation at all. Paraphrases make no effort to match the literal wording of the original Hebrew or Greek text. Instead the author decides what he thinks the text means, then rewrites it in his own words, using as many or as few words as he thinks is needed.

This leads to a Bible version that is very easy to read, a feature which makes it very popular. Because of this, paraphrases are great for children and can be a useful tool for introducing young readers to the Bible. However, just as you would not rely on an incomplete children's Bible story book for study, it is very dangerous to rely on a paraphrase as your main Bible version.

Since the author of a paraphrase (he is not a translator) looks at the thoughts of the original text in an attempt to capture the essence of each passage, he does not translate the actual words of the text itself. This results in a highly inaccurate Bible version, which may be an adequate choice for devotional reading, but it will be an especially poor choice for serious Bible study.

The Living Bible

The first major paraphrase was the Living Bible, published in 1971. Kenneth Taylor first created it as a Bible to read to his own children, yet it became immensely popular in the 1970's and 80's. Despite its popularity, it is often criticized for adding too much commentary to the biblical text.

The Message

The next major paraphrase to appear was the Message, written by Eugene Peterson and completed in 2002. Peterson takes great liberties with words in his attempt to effectively communicate both the original thoughts and tone of the Scripture. The result is a very earthy, informal language, but also a very unreliable Bible version.

The Passion "Translation"

Another popular paraphrase that has recently begun to emerge is the so-called Passion Translation. I say "so-called" because it's actually a paraphrase, not a translation. The Passion Paraphrase takes verses of Scripture and literally re-words them to include things like "prophetic singing," the "transference of the anointing," and the issuing of "apostolic decrees," which, though these may all be scripturally valid principles, they never actually appear in the original text of the verses that include those words.

Consider this example from Galatians 2:19, where the Greek *hina theō zēsō,* which simply means *"that I might live for God,"* has been rendered as *"so that I can live for God in heaven's freedom."* There is no word for either "heaven" or "freedom" in the Greek text of that sentence. Those two words do not appear in the original Greek at all. It's simply not an accurate translation into English. It's an addition to the text. There are dozens of examples like this in the Passion Paraphrase, and, according to James 3:1 and Revelation 22:18-19, Christian teachers will answer to God for re-writing and changing His Word like this.

A man named Brian Simmons, who claims the title of Apostle within the New Apostolic Reformation (NAR) movement, is the Lead Translator, which is also a questionable title, since 'Lead Translator' implies a team of translators, yet he is the only one doing the translating (actually paraphrasing). Brian Simmons says our current translations of the Bible, which (as you have already learned in the previous chapters of this book) were transcribed by hundreds of scholars over many centuries, are all just "head knowledge which can never capture God's passion."

While this all sounds very exciting, it contradicts 2 Timothy 3:16, where the Apostle Paul stated every word of the Scriptures was breathed out by the Holy Spirit Himself. Furthermore, Simmons claims his Passion Paraphrase is more authentic because it's translated from 5th century Aramaic manuscripts, but he doesn't reveal to his readers that those Aramaic sources are actually just translations of older and more reliable 2nd century Greek manuscripts.

I can't see into Brian Simmons' heart and I would never presume to question his motives, but the end result of the Passion Paraphrase is the same as every other paraphrase: an interesting, but re-worded Bible version that is not faithful to the original Greek and Hebrew texts. I would have no objection to the Passion Paraphrase if that's what he called his work, but he is misleading Bible readers when he presents it as though it were an actual translation.

I do understand how Bible versions like the Passion Paraphrase are exciting and fun to read, and while you can certainly use a paraphrase if you want, you will truly be so much better off in your Bible study efforts with a real Bible translation. As for me, I will stick to the many good, high-quality Bible versions that are available. I might use a Paraphrase occasionally, but never as my primary Bible version.

Next Steps

What's the next step? Knowing the three types of Bible translations will really help you narrow down your choice of Bible for personal use. Serious Bible students will want a Formal Equivalence translation, but if you're more of a devotional Bible reader, then you'll probably be happier with a Dynamic Equivalence version.

Once you decide what TYPE of translation you want, how can you decide on the version you'll use? Do you have to spend a ton of money on Bibles in order to find out what you don't like? Should you stand in a Christian book store for a few hours flipping through all of the available Bible versions until you find one that suits you?

I have good news for you: In the next section of this chapter I'm going to show you some Bible study tools that will allow you to check out as many different Bible versions as you want, absolutely free! Once you learn how to do that, you'll be able to compare and contrast the different Bible versions until you find the one that's right for you.

Bible Study Tool #10
Bible Study Software and Online Resources

I love holding a Bible in my hands, and I treasure my Bible collection. However, there are some awesome Bible software programs and online resources available now that allow you to get so much more studying done in a short amount of time. I want to share my five favorite programs with you today, and also some great websites that will increase the efficiency of your Bible study time.

(Reminder: I'm not affiliated with any of these sites or products, and I will make no money if you should happen to purchase any of them. This allows me to give you honest recommendations that you can trust.)

Bible Software

Most Bible software includes various Bible versions, along with digital versions of many Bible study tools such as concordances, commentaries, atlases, etc. with fully searchable content. Most programs are modular, with a lower priced base program which can be upgraded to more expensive ones.

Logos
www.logos.com

Logos is THE standard for Bible study software. It is the most expensive, with eight packages priced from $295 for the basic Starter edition up to $10,900 for the Collector's edition. Logos works on both PC and Mac. Logos offers so much that the sheer scope of the software can be intimidating to some users, but there are many instructional videos and tutorials on their site.

This software is a big investment, but each edition contains hundreds of resources that would cost many times more if you bought the print editions. There are payment plans available for all versions, and an academic discount is also offered. My brother owns Logos and he's been very happy with it. Logos also makes a free Bible app that works on PC and Mac.

PC Study Bible
www.Biblesoft.com

Biblesoft's PC Study Bible is a powerful and affordable program, with library options beginning in price from the very reasonable $90 for the starter New Reference Library to $850 for the Professional Series version. Both PC and Mac versions are available, but they do not offer payment plans.

This software includes many Bible-based commentaries and reference works. It includes the helpful Englishman's Concordance, a kind of reverse Strong's that lists every verse containing a particular Strong's number. Another really cool feature is their Biblesoft Authoring System, which allows you to create your own Bible study materials that can be integrated back into the software.

This is the Bible study software that I currently use, and while I've been satisfied with it overall, they have not kept up with the market technologically as much as I would have liked. The next time I decide to spend money for Bible study software, I will probably go with Logos.

Accordance
www.accordanceBible.com

If you're a Mac user, then Accordance Bible Software

is for you. Their software packages are geared for all levels of students, from the Starter Collection at $60 up to the Platinum Collection for $2,000. Payment plans are available, and they offer extensive training and tutorials.

An Intel processor and OS X 10.6 or later are required to run Accordance. They do have a Windows version, but the Interface still looks like a Mac program, as do most original Apple programs that are ported to Windows. However, dedicated Mac users may prefer this native Mac software to Logos or Biblesoft.

e-Sword
www.e-sword.net

e-Sword is the original free Bible software, offering much more than you'd normally expect from a free program. e-Sword includes several free add-on Bible versions, dictionaries, and commentaries. It has been downloaded over 30 million times in 235 countries around the world!

It's easy to use with tutorials, manuals, and training demos all provided on their website. While it is much more limited compared to the paid-for Bible software programs, e-Sword is a great place to start if those products are currently out of your price range.

theWord
www.theword.net

theWord software is amazing. It is fast and responsive with a fully configurable user interface. The software is designed for Windows, but users have been able to run it on Mac and Linux operating systems using Windows emulators.

You can add your own notes in theWord anywhere you want, and it is fully portable so you can carry your favorite Bibles, books, and notes on a USB flash drive. You can also create your own add-on modules which you can share with other users.

theWord software combines the best of e-Sword's price (free) with the enhanced functionality of the high-end Bible study programs. There are many 3rd-party add-on modules available for free, and many more can be purchased for download. Online tutorials can be found on their site and there is also an active online forum where you can get your questions answered.

Bible Websites

If you can't afford Bible software right now, there are a number of free Bible study websites available that offer a surprisingly wide array of tools and resources. Here are some of my favorites:

Bible Gateway
www.biblegateway.com

Bible Gateway is almost always where I start when doing Bible research online. It's one of the best ways to look up verses, search various translations and find passages of interest. It's also one of the best ways to zero in on the meaning of a particularly challenging verse. In Bible Gateway you can quickly flip through over 50 different Bible translations to see how various scholars translated a word, or even how a paraphrase version like The Living Bible or The Message gives the sense of the passage. It's a very handy way to look at different aspects of a Bible verse.

Blue Letter Bible
www.blueletterbible.org

You can spend thousands of dollars on Bible study software to help you study the Bible in the original language, with helps to parse the verbs, see lexicon entries to define the words used, or to see cross references to other places where those words are used. Yet with the Blue Letter Bible you get 90% of that functionality for free. My favorite tool is the Concordance where you can find all the places that the same word is used elsewhere in the Bible. You can find verses quickly and easily, and there's an Advanced Bible search that comes with great tools and a lot of information. Here's how I use the Blue Letter Bible site:

First, find the search bar at the top of the home page and select the Bible verse you want to study. Then, hover your mouse over Tools beside the verse you are interested in, and click on a tool such as Interlinear. This will pull up the original language of the verse (Greek or Hebrew), along with word-by-word comparisons from the original language to English. To get more information about a word, just click on its Strong's Concordance ID number.

From there you can go to an online version of *Vine's*

Expository Dictionary, where you can get a short dictionary entry, and in the section marked Outline of Biblical Usage, you can see the different ways that word is used in the Bible. If you want to go even deeper, scroll down to the section called Thayer's Lexicon to get a very detailed definition of the word, including how the word has been used in contemporary literature outside the Bible.

Biblia.com
www.biblia.com

Biblia.com was created by Logos Bible Software, but even if you don't own the software, you can sign up for a free account and get a lot of use out of this site. When a user signs into their Logos account, they can access their reading plans from the left-hand column. That column includes four tabs which are 1) Reading plans, 2) the Library list, 3) Search tool, and 4) Notes.

The Library list includes a number of free reference works, but if the user already owns Logos Bible Software, then all of the reference books associated with her Logos account will also appear there. The main part of the Biblia screen includes two window panes. You can open books in either side, so for example you could have a Bible version in one column and a commentary on the right. These can be synced to the same verse to make studying easier. Logos promises more advanced tools are coming soon.

Bible Hub
www.biblehub.com

BibleHub.com is the home of the Online Parallel

Bible Project. The interface may seem cluttered at first, but it's a very useful site with lots of resources. When you enter a Bible reference in the top search box, the site opens the verse in the left column using all of the translations and commentaries available. Along the right column there are helpful tools that show the context of the passage, cross references, and the *Treasury of Scripture Knowledge* entry for that verse.

Across the top of the site is a toolbar that allows you to navigate to specific passages in any of the available translations, including a large collection of modern and public domain translations. The toolbar also includes public domain commentaries which can be accessed via drop down lists. With the toolbar buttons, many of the tools are just a click away. There's a parallel Bible button, cross references, and a context button that shows the verse within the context of the passage. Bible Hub also includes pictures, maps, and outlines. Like the other sites listed, Bible Hub allows you to share to various social media platforms.

Bible Study Tools
www.biblestudytools.com

This site is another good option for Bible students. Users can search the Bible, read it, create daily Bible reading plans, and share Scripture using copy & paste or links that post to many popular social media platforms. Bible Study Tools adds some public domain reference tools such as commentaries, dictionaries, the International Standard Bible Encyclopedia, Old and New Testament Greek lexicons, and classic sermons from the past.

Bible Study Tools includes a number of modern and public domain Bible translations, along with some limited original language study. If you sign up for a free account, you can record user notes and highlight Bible passages on the site, allowing you to mark up the Bible within your profile and save your research for future reference.

Bible Apps

Today, good Bible study software is no longer limited to your computer. There is a wide variety of Bible study apps that you can use on your smartphone or tablet. Some Bible apps cost a small amount of money, but here are some that are free:

Faithlife Study Bible App
Platform: iOS, Android, Kindle Fire
File Size: 121 MB

This free digital study Bible includes many different Bible versions and has some very in-depth study notes and Bible study tools. There are daily devotions you can follow and reading plans that will track your progress. Additional features such as groups, news, and more, are available from the Faithlife community.

Blue Letter Bible
Platform: iOS only
File Size: 43 MB

Like their website, the Blue Letter Bible app is incredibly comprehensive. Simply select a verse, and immediately you'll have the option of looking up the

Strong's numbers for each word, as well as a host of other resources right at your fingertips. Some of the features do require an Internet connection, and it's only available for iOS, but other than that it's everything you would expect with the name Blue Letter Bible.

Logos Bible App
Platform: iOS, Android, Kindle Fire, PC, Mac
File Size: 45 MB

With the Logos Bible app, you open up more than 40 free Bibles and over 70 other free books. When you sign in with a free Logos account, you get access to additional resources and tools, such as devotionals, reading plans, favorites, highlighting, and note taking. You can create and connect with private groups, and if you're already a Logos customer, you can quickly download any resources that you own. An Internet connection is required to access the books, but that also helps keep the file size down so it takes up less space on your device.

Olive Tree Bible+
Platform: iOS, Android
File Size: 60 MB

Olive Tree Bible+ has all of the features other Bible apps have, but it has the cleanest, most readable interface of them all. The app intuitively allows you to highlight with customized highlighters, take notes with customized fonts and varying text sizes, and change the font and color schemes to whatever you find the most readable. You can even set the gestures to make it easier to navigate the app and customize it to your reading habits. If you're looking for a basic Bible app that you can completely customize, Olive Tree Bible+ will work for you.

Bible.is
Platform: iOS, Android
File Size: 14MB

Bible.is offers a wide array of options and is the hub of an impressive network of Bible apps. It's easy to read, study, and share God's Word with friends and family around the world. You can also hear the Bible brought to life in high quality, dramatized audio, perfect for walking or listening in the car. With JESUS Film integration, you can see the Scriptures come to life in a truly immersive Bible experience. Whether you're a Pastor, teacher, or student, this app will be useful to you.

There are many, many, more online Bible study sites. I've only scratched the surface here. Today we are so blessed to have such free access to the Word of God. I encourage you to make the most of it.

Bible Study Method #10
Chapter Analysis Study
(The Expository Method)

Expository Bible study is also sometimes referred to as inductive Bible study. It is the opposite of a topical Bible study, which gathers verses on a single topic from all over the Bible. Instead, the expository Bible study method focuses on a single passage of text. Usually this is a single Bible chapter, but it could also be a complete story that is only a part of a chapter.

You may have heard the term expository sermon, in which a minister preaches from only a single passage of text, rather than jumping all over the Bible preaching about a specific topic, which is called a topical sermon. The objective of an expository sermon, and of expository Bible study, is to "expose" what the text is actually saying to us.

The Chapter Analysis Study picks up where the Book Survey Study ends. Now that you have a good grasp of the overall picture of the book, what it means, why it was written, and so forth, you can begin to examine the individual parts that make up the book. The best way of subdividing a book of the Bible is to use the existing chapter divisions and study each chapter in detail. You will examine paragraphs, sentences, and words following a systematic and detailed plan.

The Chapter Analysis Study is the second of three methods of Bible study that, when taken together, will give you an in-depth view of a particular book of the Bible. These three methods are a lot of work, but they also reveal the greatest results. You will need your usual kit of Bible reference tools on hand for this study, including several Bible translations, Bible dictionaries, encyclopedias, handbooks, Bible commentaries, and Old and New Testament surveys. Here are the steps for a Chapter Analysis Study:

Step 1 – Create a chapter summary

First read the chapter several times through. After

you have done that, describe the content of the chapter, and find a way of summarizing it using one of the following methods:

Outline the chapter

Create an outline of the chapter based on the internal paragraph divisions in the chapter. Give each paragraph a heading and put any sub-points within the paragraph underneath it. This is similar to the outline you made in the Book Survey study last chapter, but this time it's only for the single chapter.

Rewrite the chapter

When you rewrite it, leave out any modifying clauses or phrases. Use only the subjects, verbs, and objects. This can be challenging, but the result is a vastly simplified record of what happened in the chapter.

Paraphrase the chapter

Rephrase the chapter in your own words. This should be done in a way that would allow another person to clearly understand it.

Step 2 – Observation: What does this passage say?

The next step in exposing the text is to simply observe it. Try to let go of any presuppositions you might have about the passage in question. Don't try to force the text into your own teaching outline. Instead, let the outline of the passage emerge naturally from the text as you observe it. To help you observe the passage, ask the standard questions a news reporter would ask: Who is involved? What happened? What was taught? When? Where? How? Why? This will allow you to discover what the author is trying to say.

Record your observations and insights. Look at every detail of the chapter, examining each sentence and word, and writing down everything you see. Look for any key words or repeated words or phrases in the passage. See if you can find any warnings or commands. Here is a list of things you should look for:

- Key words
- Repeated words and phrases
- Questions being asked
- Answers being given
- Commands
- Warnings
- Comparisons - things that are alike
- Contrasts - things that are different
- Illustrations
- Causes and effects for why things happen
- Motivations causing characters to take certain actions
- Promises and their conditions for fulfillment
- Progression from the general to the specific or from the specific to the general
- Steps of progression in a narrative or biography
- Lists of things
- Advice or admonitions

• The tone of the passage - attitudes and emotional atmosphere
• Explanations
• Old Testament quotes in the New Testament
• References to current events in the time it was written

Pray to God and ask for the Holy Spirit's guidance. Slowly read the passage over and over again, turning it over in your mind. Look at the passage in different Bible versions and see what else you notice.

Step 3 – Interpretation: What does this passage mean?

Ask detailed questions of the chapter. What is the author's intent in this passage? What is the major principle or lesson which the writer (and the God who inspired him) wanted to communicate? How was his message relevant to his audience, the people of that day? How would they have understood what he was saying?

Take note of each question you ask, even if you aren't able to find the answer right away. The time may come when you find the answer during another study and then you'll be able to place it here as well.

Observe the context of the passage

If you've already done a Book Survey Study for this book, that will be helpful to you here.

Define the words and phrases used

Make use of your Bible reference tools to insure that you have the correct understanding of the key words and phrases within the passage. Use a Bible dictionary to define any unfamiliar words or ideas.

Look at the structure and grammar of the passage

This can help you to understand the flow of ideas and concepts within the passage, enabling you to see how they stand in relation to each other.

Use other translations

Look at other translations to see whether they are more understandable. Often another translation will have slightly different wording that will shine a little more light on the passage.

View the passage against its background

As needed, use Bible study helps to get a clearer meaning of the passage, such as Bible dictionaries and encyclopedias, or a Bible study guide for the text, subject, or person being studied.

Refer to a commentary as a last resort

If all other means have failed, you can refer to a commentary to compare your interpretation of the passage with that of the commentator. The reason this is the last resort is because if you did it first it would inevitably bias your own interpretations as you discover them.

Once again, pray for the Holy Spirit's guidance as you think these questions through and try to determine the main idea or principle lesson of the passage. Why do you think God put this in the Bible?

Step 4 – Compare your chapter with other Bible passages

Now look at other Scriptures that relate to this passage. See what other passages in the Bible say about the concepts covered in this chapter. These are usually found in the center marginal notes of Bibles or in footnotes. What do these other related verses reveal about the author's thoughts or ideas?

Step 5 – Make a list of some potential life applications from the passage

Now look at your own life. What is the Holy Spirit saying to YOU in this passage? Ask Him and wait quietly for a moment to see what thoughts and impressions you get. Make sure you take note of anything that comes to you so it doesn't slip away later.

Next, think about your life in relation to the passage you've just studied. Ask yourself "What is one practical way I can apply the main idea of this passage to my life?" Usually more than one application idea will come to you.

Be sure you take them all down.

This is a list you are making for future reference. You will not be attempting to apply everything that you write here, but in step seven (below) you will choose one of these applications to start working into your life.

Step 6 – Draw your own conclusions

Review the first five steps of this study, then come up with some initial conclusions about the chapter and write them down. As you do this, you might discover additional connections within the chapter, which will lead to new ideas about the chapter. Take note of those as well.

Step 7 – Application – How can I apply this principle to my life?

Write down one life application from the list you made in step five. Be sure that it is both practical and applicable to your life personally. Remember to return to your written application in the near future so you can evaluate your progress.

Finally, consider your attitude and your actions. What will you do differently based on what you've learned? It doesn't have to be some huge mountain-moving thing. Most of the time spiritual growth is very gradual and hardly noticeable when it's happening. Only later when you look back and realize how far you've come will you recognize how God was helping you along the whole time.

These are the steps for a Chapter Analysis Study that will allow you to expose the treasures that are buried within the text of a Bible passage. Topical studies can be useful and definitely have their place, but nothing is as profitable as dealing directly and in-depth with a specific text from God's Word.

Another advantage of expository studies is you don't have to be "feeling it" first in order to get into a good session of Bible study. The text is the text, and you can look at it and analyze it whether you're feeling spiritual at the moment or not. When you do this, you'll find that what will usually happen is the discipline of studying will actually motivate you into a more spiritual mood.

Finally, while an expository study can be focused on a shorter passage or story contained within a chapter, this is also the best study method to use for chapter studies. When you can break down an entire Bible chapter using the expository study method, you'll see links between the stories within the chapter that you may have missed before. There's a reason the author put his book in that particular order, and when you start to make those connections, new revelation and insight that you've never seen before will be opened up to you.

Summary

There are three different types of Bible translations: formal equivalence, dynamic equivalence, and paraphrases, which are not actually translations at all. Formal equivalence translations are the most faithful word-for-word translations from the Hebrew and Greek texts into English, but because the translation is so exact, reading it in English can sound choppy and disjointed.

Dynamic equivalence translations are more thought-for-thought than word-for-word, so they are easier to read in English, but the translation from the original languages is not as precise. There are varying degrees of dynamic equivalence translations, including intermediate dynamic equivalence and functional dynamic equivalence.

If you think of Bible translations as a spectrum, intermediate dynamic equivalence translations are closer to formal equivalence versions, while functional dynamic equivalence translations tend to be more towards the opposite end of the spectrum, closer to paraphrase versions.

We live in a day of awesome privileges and blessings. It's hard to believe there was a time when the only copy of the Bible in a town was chained to the pulpit in the town's church, and the authorities hunted down unauthorized copies of the Bible so they could destroy them.

Today, at least in the English speaking world, we have free access not only to the Word of God in dozens of different translations, but also nearly infinite access to powerful Bible study software and online tools, many of which are available for free. Praise God!

Finally, we looked at the Chapter Analysis study method, sometimes referred to as the expository method, especially when the passage in question is less than one chapter. The expository Bible study method focuses on a single passage of text, usually a single Bible chapter or a complete story contained within a chapter.

Since expository studies deal only with a single passage of text, they are easier to begin than other Bible study methods. However, a successful expository study will "expose" the text, allowing you to dig deep into the passage and pull out all kinds of nuggets of revelation and wisdom.

The Chapter Analysis study is the second of three study methods that together will give you the greatest understanding of a particular book of the Bible. The first was the Book Survey Study, which was covered in chapter 9, and the third is the Book Synthesis Study, which we will cover in the next chapter.

Chapter 10 Discussion Questions

1. Have you decided on a specific Bible version that you will use for study purposes? What factors influenced your decision?

2. A word-for-word translation with great attention paid to the original text's grammatical structure is what type of Bible translation?

3. What type of Bible translation is more of a thought-for-thought interpretation, reworded in order to better convey the meaning of the original writer?

4. What are the advantages and disadvantages of formal equivalence and dynamic equivalence translations?

5. How are Bible paraphrases different from actual Bible translations? What are some of the dangers of relying too heavily on a paraphrased Bible version? In what ways could a Bible paraphrase be helpful?

6. Dynamic equivalence translations can be divided into intermediate and functional. Which one is closer to formal equivalence translations? Which is closer to a paraphrase?

7. Technology helps us to learn and store information, making it very useful for Bible study. What are some possible drawbacks to using technology in Bible study? What are the drawbacks to using books and paper?

8. When doing a Chapter study, at what point should you consult a Bible commentary? Why?

Chapter 11

Transformed

Internalizing the Word of God

Don't let the world around you squeeze you into its own mold, but let God re-mold your minds from within, so that you may prove in practice that the plan of God for you is good, meets all his demands and moves towards the goal of true maturity. - Romans 12:2 (PHL)

It's time to tie together everything that has been covered so far in *How To Study Your Bible*. We've looked at the history of the Bible and why there are so many different translations available today. Now we're going to introduce the art of meditating on the Word of God, look at creating your own study Bible, and wrap up the Bible study methods.

Meditating God's Word

I've found that one of the best Bible study tools is your own imagination. Learning to direct your imagination toward godly things will give you the ability to meditate on God's Word. We are used to thinking of our imagination in a negative sense, because so often our imagination is focused on negative things like lust, envy, jealousy, or revenge. However, our imagination is really just one part of the mind God created in us, and we can direct it toward good or evil.

When it comes to spiritual warfare, the Bible teaches us that the mind is the battlefield where the vast majority of that conflict takes place. The Apostle Paul wrote:

> **For though we walk in the flesh, we do not war after the flesh: (For the weapons of our warfare are not carnal, but mighty through God to the pulling down of strong holds;) Casting down imaginations, and every high thing that exalteth itself against the knowledge of God, and bringing into captivity every thought to the obedience of Christ;**
> **- 2 Corinthians 10:3-5 (KJV)**

We aren't supposed to let our imaginations run unchecked with sinful thoughts, because doing so will only lead to sinful actions. "For as a man thinketh in his heart, so is he" (Proverbs 23:7). But did it ever occur to you that you can direct your imagination toward godly thoughts? That's what meditating the Word of God is about. Like devotional reading, meditating the Word isn't really a Bible Study method, but it's something you should do every day.

> **This Book of the Law shall not depart from your mouth, but you shall meditate in it day and night, that you may observe to do according to all that is written in it. For then you will make**

**your way prosperous, and then you will have
good success. - Joshua 1:8 (NKJ)**

Meditating God's Word isn't like the meditation
of Eastern religions. In New Age thinking, meditation
involves emptying your mind of all thoughts in the hopes of
somehow reaching a point of enlightenment, but Bible
meditation is completely the opposite. The fact of the
matter is that all false spiritual teachings have a grain
of truth in them. That's what makes their lies so effective,
Meditating on God's Word means you are filling your mind
up with the Word of God, not emptying it out.

**1 Blessed [fortunate, prosperous, and favored
by God] is the man who does not walk in the
counsel of the wicked [following their advice
and example], nor stand in the path of sinners,
nor sit [down to rest] in the seat of scoffers
(ridiculers).
2 But his delight is in the law of the Lord, <u>and on
His law [His precepts and teachings] he [habitu-
ally] meditates day and night</u>.
3 And he will be like a tree firmly planted [and
fed] by streams of water, Which yields its fruit
in its season; Its leaf does not wither; And in
whatever he does, he prospers [and comes to
maturity]. - Psalm 1:1-3 (AMP)**

So how does meditating the Word of God work? How
do you set your imagination to work in a positive direction
toward thinking godly thoughts? There are two ways
that I've discovered to do it. The Hebrew word translated
"meditate" in Joshua 1:8 and Psalm 1:2 literally means

"muttering under your breath," which is the first way to meditate God's Word.

For example, say you wanted to meditate on Philippians 4:19, which says "But my God shall supply all your need according to his riches in glory by Christ Jesus." How should you go about muttering Philippians 4:19 under your breath all day? I would take one word in the verse and emphasize it as I muttered that verse. Then I would emphasize the next word, and so forth.

Doing this can also open up to you more of the revelation that's contained in the verse. The living Word of God is infinite, and you will never get it all in this life. There's always more light, there's always another layer, there's always another nugget buried in that verse. But meditating on the Word by muttering can open a verse up to you in ways you've never seen before.

As you do this, you don't have to be weird about it. Talk under your breath if you're at work or around people who won't understand what you're doing, but if you're free to speak aloud then go ahead and do that. Let me show you what I mean. If you happened to be standing next to me while I was doing this, it would sound like this:

- **BUT** *my God shall supply all your need according to his riches in glory by Christ Jesus.*
- *But* **MY** *God shall supply all your need according to his riches in glory by Christ Jesus.*
- *But my* **GOD** *shall supply all your need according to his riches in glory by Christ Jesus.*
- *But my God* **SHALL** *supply all your need*

according to his riches in glory by Christ Jesus.

And so forth. Notice how emphasizing each word of the verse brings a new meaning out of the words:

* ***BUT*** *my God shall supply all your need*
  according to his riches in glory by Christ Jesus.

"But" is a connecting word. You don't end a sentence with the word "but." It means there's something coming after it. The story isn't over yet!

* *But* **MY** *God shall supply all your need*
  according to his riches in glory by Christ Jesus.

This is MY God we're talking about. This isn't some distant, far away God, but the One with whom I have a personal relationship.

* *But my* ***GOD*** *shall supply all your need*
  according to his riches in glory by Christ Jesus.

This is the One True God we're talking about here. Not some false god, not some namby-pamby god, but MY God – the Creator of Heaven and Earth, who cannot lie and cannot fail!

* *But my God* **SHALL** *supply all your need*
  according to his riches in glory by Christ Jesus.

He didn't say "I might." He didn't say "Perhaps." He didn't say "Maybe." He said my God SHALL supply! It's not a possibility. It's a promise! Praise God!

> **My mouth shall speak** wisdom; **the meditation**
> **of my heart** shall be understanding.
>   **- Psalm 49:3**

I'm sure you can see the benefit of meditating God's Word by "muttering" a Bible verse like this over and over again throughout your day. Not only will it inspire your faith, but it will also help you with memorizing verses. I thought about including a section in this book on how to memorize Scriptures, but the truth of the matter is, if you can get a verse down on the inside of you, memorization happens as a by-product of that process.

Another way to use your God-given imagination to meditate on the Word is to visualize yourself as a character in a particular Bible story. Now, visualization is another of those words that the New Age movement has hijacked. That's why Christians sometimes get tense when you talk about it, but what they don't realize is the New Agers stole it from the Bible! Jesus Himself said,

> **So Jesus said to them, "Truly, truly, I say to you,**
> **the Son can do nothing of his own accord, but**
> **only what he SEES the Father doing. For whatever**
> **the Father does, that the Son does likewise."**
>   **- John 5:19 (ESV)**

While a full study on scriptural visualization is beyond the scope of this work, the Bible is full of verses telling us what to look at and what to avoid looking at, both in the real world and in our minds. Therefore, we are well within the bounds of good doctrine and practice when it comes to visualizing the Scriptures through meditation on the Word of God.

I will <u>meditate on your precepts</u> and <u>fix my eyes</u> on your ways. - Psalm 119:15

Now, let's look at an example. Mark 2:1-12 tells the story of the paralyzed man who was carried by four of his friends to the house where Jesus was teaching so that Jesus could heal him. When they arrived, they found there were so many people crowded around the house that the only way they could get to Jesus was to climb up on the roof, tear part of it off, and then lower their friend down to where Jesus was! Jesus healed him of course, and then the Pharisees criticized Him, and Jesus dealt with that. It's one of my favorite Bible stories because of how it illustrates not quitting on your faith. Take a moment to read the story now, and then we'll meditate on this passage together.

Okay, you've read the story, now close your eyes and picture the scene. Jesus is teaching in the house, and there are people everywhere! Now we're going to imagine what it looked like from the perspective of each character in the story, starting with the four friends carrying the paralyzed man.

In your mind, make yourself one of the four friends. Your good friend is paralyzed. Earlier you heard that Jesus was going to be nearby, so you and three of your friends got together and decided to take your friend to Jesus to be healed. Now you are here and you can't get through. What are you thinking? What are you feeling? Then, as your eyes trace upward to the roof, a really crazy idea comes to you.

How do you talk your friends into climbing on the

roof with you? How do you feel when you're all up there ripping out a hole big enough to lower your friend through? How awkward does it feel looking down into the room at Jesus and your friend? How amazing does it feel when you see your friend get up and walk out on his own? After you climb back down, what do you say to him? Finally, how are you going to make amends for the broken roof?

Now be a nameless face in the crowd. You're standing just outside the house, straining to see Jesus inside and hear what He is teaching. Behind you four men arrive carrying a stretcher. You chuckle to yourself because there's no way they're going to get through this press of people while carrying that man. They should have been here much earlier. You forget about them and lean in close to the window so you can hear Jesus better. You don't want to miss a word.

Suddenly, dust starts coming down from the ceiling onto Jesus' head, right in the middle of His teaching! You look up and see someone tearing a hole in the roof. It's those four men! How dare they tear up this man's house? What a bunch of jerks! You watch them lower their friend down and see Jesus heal him. The man was paralyzed but now he's standing and walking! Jesus is so awesome, and that man's four friends? They are heroes! They didn't let anything stop them from getting their friend the help he needed! That's how I picture being a face in that crowd. What do you see when you imagine yourself there? What do you feel?

Now be the paralyzed friend. You've been paralyzed for so long, but you have hope because you've heard about this Jesus. You're so thankful for your four friends who have been good enough to take you to where Jesus is. Then you get there and see all the people. How do you feel? Does your heart sink? Does hope turn to even greater discouragement? But wait, now your friends are talking. What are they saying? The roof? What? The next thing you know, you're being hoisted up onto the roof of the house. How do you feel lying on your stretcher while your friends carry you up so high? And now they're tearing up the roof! How do you feel now? Are you embarrassed? Do you wonder if you're worth all this trouble? Maybe you don't know what to think. Now what? Whoa! What are they doing? They're interrupting Jesus' teaching, lowering you down into the house, landing your stretcher right in front of Jesus and the entire crowd.

How do you feel? Do you try to curl up and hide, even though you're paralyzed? Do you look up at your friends through the hole in the roof and imagine giving them a few choice words when this is over? Are you nervous to be before Jesus, to have Him looking right at you? Then He reaches forth His hand and tells you that your sins are forgiven and to rise up and walk. Suddenly, for the first time in a long, long time, you have the strength to stand on your own! You take one careful step, then another, then another, gaining confidence with each passing step. You are healed! The crowd goes crazy. Jesus and the Pharisees are arguing about something, but who cares? You can walk! How does it feel to be walking after being paralyzed for so long? What do you say to Jesus? What do you say to your friends?

Now be one of the Pharisees. What does it mean to be you? You are recognized as a religious leader in your community, but now this travelling prophet has come around stirring everyone up. Are you envious of His popularity? Do you feel your position is threatened by His radical teaching? Or are you curious to hear what He has to say so you can find out what all the fuss is about? Maybe it's a combination of all of these feelings. As you sit and listen to Him teach, you feel thankful that your high office allows you to be seated comfortably inside the house, just a few feet away from Jesus. What do you think about the crowd outside that couldn't get in? How do you feel about them?

Suddenly, there's a noise from the ceiling, and you look up to see four men lowering another man down on a stretcher. How dare they do this! Not only are they destroying property and embarrassing you in front of all these people, but their destructive behavior has interrupted Jesus' teaching! Then you hear Jesus tell the man, "Your sins are forgiven you." This is an outrage! You and all of your Pharisee friends immediately protest, because only God can forgive sin. Then Jesus says, "Which is easier, to say your sins are forgiven or to say to this man, rise, take up your bed and walk? But so you will know the Son of Man has power to forgive sins..." Jesus looks down at the paralyzed man lying before Him and says, "Rise, take up your bed and walk." And he does! The crowd goes insane praising and glorifying God, while you are left there, exchanging nervous glances with the other Pharisees. How do you feel at this point? What would you secretly like to tell Jesus? What does your pride and your fear allow you to say to your fellow religious leaders instead? Are you feeling tension? Why?

Now imagine you are Jesus. Obviously we can never "be" Jesus, because He was fully man and fully God, but we know He set aside His divine attributes and was born into the earth so that God would be able to relate to us (Hebrews 4:15). So imagine you're Jesus, identifying with the human side of Him, not to be irreverent at all, but just to help you get a better sense of what happened that day. The Holy Spirit has led you into this town to teach the Word of God, and you've been welcomed into this house with honor. Before you, the most prestigious religious leaders from the area are seated, while behind them and packed all around the house are the rest of the people. How do you feel about both groups? Then, as you're in the middle of your message, there's a commotion above you. Someone is lowering a stretcher down to you! Everyone is stunned, but you just go with it.

When the man on the stretcher is set down in front of you, it suddenly comes to you just what to say. You know the Pharisees won't like it, but you also know your Father God will back you up all the way. "Your sins are forgiven you," you say to the paralyzed man. As you expected, the Pharisees erupt in protests. Then you say, "Which is easier, to say your sins are forgiven or to say to this man, rise, take up your bed and walk? But so you will know the Son of Man has power to forgive sins..."

You look down at the paralyzed man lying before you and say, "Rise, take up your bed and walk." God works a miracle as you knew He would, and the man rises up. The crowd bursts forth with praise to God, and the Pharisees are silenced for the moment. How do you feel? Thankful for the man? Impressed with the faith of his four friends? Happy to see the people glorifying God? Sad for the Pharisees? What about the rest of your teaching? What will you do next?

**May my meditation be pleasing to him, for I
rejoice in the Lord. - Psalm 104:34**

This method of meditating on the Word of God will
bring the Bible to life for you. Using your God-given
imagination, you can visualize yourself as each of the
characters in any Bible story. This will not only make those
stories feel more real to you, but it will also allow you to
recognize certain interpersonal connections between the
characters that you might otherwise have overlooked,
because imagining yourself in the role of each character
in this way engages not only your mind, but also your
emotions.

Meditating God's Word is also a great way to focus
your mind when you go to sleep at night, especially if the
enemy is trying to bombard you with fear and anxiety.
If the devil is going to disrupt your sleep, you can make
him pay for it by spending that time lying awake in bed
meditating on God's Word instead of concentrating on the
junk he wants you to think about.

**My eyes are awake before the watches of the
night, that I may meditate on your promise.
- Psalm 119:148**

Bible Study Tool #11
Creating Your Own Study Bible

By now you've hopefully settled on a Bible translation
to use as your main version. You might even be starting to
explore different study Bibles and other tools. One thing

you'll find out right away is that the cost of Bibles and study materials can add up quickly! Another thing I've discovered is that the quality of many Bible study books today has decreased, to the point that I'm often shocked and disappointed at what my local Christian book store has to offer.

A handful are excellent, but many supposed study Bibles have only a few little boxes that contain devotional notes and comments, and especially, I'm sorry to say, if they bear the name of some celebrity pastor. Like me, you may also find yourself dissatisfied with the study Bibles that are available, and if that's the case, then your answer may be to create your own study Bible.

Now, if you're the type of person who thinks that making marks or writing in your Bible is sacrilegious, and the thought of doing so horrifies you, go ahead and skip to the next section, because this won't work for you. However, if the idea of creating a personalized study Bible is something that stirs your interest, then keep reading!

My First Original Study Bible

In the early 90's I worked part-time in the copy center of a Christian university. I was unsatisfied with what was available in stores at the time, because there were no Bibles with wide margins, or if there were I couldn't find them because there was no Internet yet! So, on my own time and at my own expense, I decided to create my own study Bible.

(Warning: The following paragraph contains graphic violence which may offend some readers!)

I tore the binding off of my Thompson Chain Reference Bible and separated all of the Bible pages. Then I made an 8.5"x 11" frame on white cardstock with a hole cut in the center that perfectly fit the two columns and center reference of each Bible page. I taped the cardstock to the glass on the copier and painstakingly put the first page in the frame, copied it, flipped it over, copied the other side, and then moved on to the next page of the Bible.

I repeated this process for weeks, coming in early every morning, eventually working my way through the entire Bible until I had my own master copy. The letter-sized pages had plenty of room for my notes, and I used the industrial drill at the copy center to punch holes in the pages so I could store them in 3-ring binders. The Old Testament filled three binders, with one more for the New Testament.

A few years later I created version 2 of my study Bible, which I jokingly referred to as the OCD version. I used Microsoft Publisher, setting up the pages the same way, meticulously cutting and pasting the text of the King James into the columns, and then printing the pages 2-sided. That's how much I wanted to create my own study Bible. Thankfully, you won't have to work anywhere near that hard today!

Get A Wide Margin Bible

If you want to create your own study Bible, the first thing you'll need is a wide margin Bible. I suggest you purchase the best one you can afford, since higher quality

Bibles will last longer. This will be a Bible you'll use extensively, and it could even be handed down to future generations, which is another reason you want high quality.

Now that there is more of a demand for this type of Bible, there are many good wide-margin Bibles available. The *ESV Journaling Bible* is a Bible combined with an attractive Moleskin Notebook. Each page has a single column of text and wide outside margins with lines for easy note taking. Crossway publishes the *ESV Wide Margin*, with a double-column paragraph format. It has 1" margins, but no center cross reference.

I personally use the *KJV Concord Wide-Margin Reference Bible* by Cambridge. It has wide inner and outer margins, a center cross-reference, several blank ruled pages in the back, a concordance, index, and maps. Cambridge is also the only publisher that offers wide margin Bibles in all of the major translations, so if you're not a fan of the King James, you should still be able to get a wide margin Bible that will work for you.

Find the Best Writing Tools

Once you've selected your wide margin Bible, your next step is to find the proper writing tools. I usually make notes in my Bible in pencil at first so I can make changes if necessary, and then once I'm satisfied, I will erase the pencil and rewrite the note in ink.

If you use a pencil that's too sharp, it can rip the page, and if you use the wrong pen or highlighter, the color can bleed through to the next page. I recommend Pigma Micron markers. They come in .05 and .01 size points. I use .05 for underlining text and .01 for writing notes. The smaller the point, the less ink goes onto the page, and the less chance of its bleeding through. You can use the markers to color code your notes by type of note or by topic.

Mechanical pencils are another option. If you write small enough, you can fit a lot more notes in the margin, and of course, you can always erase them. However, all of your notes will be the same color, and the lead will smear when your fingers rub against it.

You can also use colored mechanical pencils, but those are better for highlighting text. Zebright makes good highlighters, and PrimsaColor and Crayola are two good options for colored pencils. If you want to mark the Bible text itself, you can either highlight it or draw a colored box around the verses.

It's a good idea to place a thin piece of cardboard under the page you're writing on. This will also help keep you from making unwanted indentations in the pages underneath. For books toward the beginning or end of the Bible, it can be challenging to get the cover to lay flat.

You can solve that problem by putting a smaller book under the cover to smooth out any bends. That way you'll be able to write without having to twist your hand into an awkward position, and you'll be able to easily write in the inner margins.

What to Write in the Margins

There are many different kinds of notes you could write in the margins of your personalized study Bible. The only real limit is your imagination. Making your own notes also improves your recollection and comprehension. You will learn the text more easily and remember it better when you interact with it directly.

Here are some ideas you might use: bible symbols, biographical facts, chain references, charts, contrasts, cultural information, dates, drawings, keywords and connecting words, lists, locations, maps, observations, parallel passages, prayers, questions, quotes, sermon outlines, themes, timelines, topical notes, word studies, and even your own commentary about the Scriptures.

Creating your own personalized study Bible is an investment, especially of your time. At first the idea of making your own study Bible might seem intimidating, but all you have to do is begin. As the saying goes, the best time to plant a tree was 20 years ago. The second best time to plant a tree is right now. Set aside some of the things in your life that don't matter, in order to free up your schedule so that you can start spending that time immersing yourself in God's Word instead.

Bible Study Method #11
Book Synthesis Study

The word synthesis means the combining of the

separate elements of material into a single or unified whole. With the Book Synthesis study, you will summarize and compact the results of your Book Survey study and your Chapter Analysis studies, putting the details you pulled from the book back together again.

Once again, these three methods, taken together, require a high level of effort on your part, but they will ultimately yield the most thorough results in your study of any book of the Bible. You will use the same Bible reference tools you used in the previous two Bible study methods, along with your Book Survey and Chapter Analysis studies that you created. You will need to refer to them often during your Book Synthesis study.

Step 1 - Reread the book several times

Do this in the same manner as you did in the Book Survey study (as described in chapter 9), taking notes as you go.

Step 2 - Write out a detailed final outline

Start with the preliminary outline from your Book Survey study, and the summaries from your Chapter Analysis studies. Combine these with the notes from your readings in step 1 to write out your outline in its final form.

Step 3 - Write a descriptive book title

To do this, use the same methods you followed to give titles to each part of your Chapter Analysis study (as described in chapter 10). Try to make the title original, defining the contents of the book in as few words as possible.

Step 4 - Make a summary of your insights

Based on what you discovered in your previous Book Survey study and Chapter Analysis studies of this book of the Bible, summarize your conclusions on the major and minor ideas of the book. Don't look at any published commentaries yet, since the goal is to arrive at your own understanding of this book of the Bible. You can also include any new ideas you discovered during your readings from step one.

Step 5 - Write out a personal application

Go back through your Book Survey study and your Chapter Analysis studies for this Bible book, and review all the personal goals and applications that your study generated. Take note of any that are still not completed, and create a plan to reach those remaining goals as soon as possible. If you were able to complete all of your personal goals and applications, look for new ones, and make a plan to implement those in your life as well.

Step 6 - Share the results of your study

Earlier in this book I suggested that as you became a more proficient Bible student, you would eventually find yourself teaching or leading Bible studies. If you've come this far and successfully stuck with it, by now you should have a solid chunk of material on the Bible book that you've been studying.

Now it's time to share the fruit of your efforts with others who share your interest in the Word of God. You may not be called to the ministry of the teacher, or to the Teacher's office (Ephesians 4:11), but that doesn't mean you can't share your new insights with those of like precious faith.

As a part of the Body of Christ (Ephesians 4:13-16; 1 Corinthians 12:12-27), you are called to minister to your fellow believers. Remember that although we are saved individually through Jesus Christ, our faith is lived out within a community. Pray to God that He will give you guidance as to when would be an appropriate time to share the things He's revealed to you.

Summary

Meditating God's Word is a way to use your God-given imagination while steering it toward the Bible rather than allowing your imagination to lead you in the other wrong directions. Bible meditation doesn't mean "emptying your mind" as it is commonly understood today. Rather it means to "fill your mind" with thoughts centered on the Word of God.

There are two main ways to meditate the Word of God. One way is to "mutter" a Bible verse under your breath, emphasizing a different word of the verse each time you say it. Another way is to take a Bible story and visualize yourself in the role of the various characters in the story. Doing this will often give you insights into why certain Bible characters thought and acted as they did, and from that you can draw lessons for your own life.

Study Bibles will help you learn more about God's Word, but a great way to really internalize the Bible is to create your own study Bible. You'll need a Bible with margins wide enough to write your study notes, and there are many good choices available. You'll also need the correct writing utensils so you don't damage your Bible's pages.

What you do with the study Bible you create is limited only by your imagination. Begin by thinking about the kinds of features and information you would like in a study Bible, and then work on making your own study Bible match your personal specifications. Creating your own study Bible will be an awesome experience for you, and it could easily become something you value enough to hand down to your loved ones someday.

The Book Synthesis method will help you combine the elements of other separate Bible studies into a unified whole. These three Bible study methods, the Book Survey, the Chapter Analysis, and now the Book Synthesis will give you a very solid understanding of any book of the Bible that you choose to study.

We started *How To Study Your Bible* with some of the more basic Bible study methods. These later chapters contain Bible study methods that take more effort and are more time consuming, but the results are worth it. You could do a Book Survey or a Chapter Analysis (or even a part of a chapter) separately and still learn many valuable things from your Bible, but when they are done in sequence, these three study methods can yield an amazing amount of information about a particular Bible book.

Chapter 11 Discussion Questions

1. One of your best Bible study tools is your:
    A) Strong's Concordance
    B) Bible Atlas
    C) Logos software
    D) Imagination

2. When is a good time for you to meditate? Is there a time of day when you can focus solely on the Word?

3. What are two ways you can meditate the Scriptures?

4. Meditating on God's Word can also:
    A) Provide deeper biblical revelation
    B) Inspire your faith
    C) Aid in Scripture memorization
    D) All of the above

5. Why would a Bible student want to create his or her own Study Bible?

6. What materials do you think would be the most useful in making your Study Bible?

7. What elements would be included in this Study Bible that you would create for yourself?

8. The Book Synthesis study combines the results of what other two Bible study methods?

9. Step 6 of the Book Synthesis study is "Share the results of your study." Why is this important for you to do?

Conclusion

"Is not My word like a fire?" says the Lord,
"And like a hammer that breaks the rock in pieces?"
- Jeremiah 23:29 (NKJ)

As you've read through the 11 chapters of this book, my hope is that you now feel empowered to embrace the Word of God as a Bible student in your own right. Yes, we still need anointed pastors and teachers, and God has set them in the church for our benefit, but at the same time you don't have to be dependent on any man or woman to become a student of the Bible.

By now you should also be well on your way to developing a Bible student mentality, where learning the Bible is not an event, but a process. You understand that the rest of your time here on Earth (and possibly in Heaven as well if you don't get it figured out down here!) will be an ongoing Bible study experience that will allow you to mine the treasures of wisdom and revelation from God's Word.

I really mean it when I say this will be for the rest of your life. When I shared an early draft of *How To Study Your Bible* with one of my friends, he said it is really two books in one. The material contained in this book is very dense and concentrated. You won't master it in a week, or a month, or a year. Bible study is incredibly rewarding, but it's not for the spiritually lazy.

However, if you put the work in, and lean on the teaching ministry of the Holy Spirit along the way, you'll be amazed at the progress you will make. If you're smart, you'll take advantage of the insights that others have found in God's Word, even as you share your own revelations and discoveries. Look for people who share your passion for Bible study, because iron sharpens iron (Proverbs 27:17).

Finally, I want to share one last Bible study tool that will serve you well throughout your entire journey as a Bible student: humility. Be very cautious not to allow pride to seep into your consciousness with all of this new Bible knowledge you're obtaining. The most highly educated man of the New Testament, the Apostle Paul, said:

...knowledge puffs up, but love builds up. If anyone imagines that he knows something, he does not yet know as he ought to know. But if anyone loves God, he is known by God.
- 1 Corinthians 8:1b-3

Nobody likes to be around a know-it-all, so make sure you don't come across that way to people. If you follow the steps covered in this book, you will become extremely knowledgeable about the Bible in a very short time. As you learn, you will also begin to realize how much you still don't know, but relative to so many of the people around you, you will be the local Bible expert.

Always remember it's not about the knowledge, it's about the love. As you increase more and more in knowledge about the Bible, the enemy will tempt you with pride. Think about it: what better way for Satan to short-circuit your spiritual gains than to start whispering in your ear how awesome you are because of how much Bible knowledge you now possess?

But love builds up! Take that knowledge, revelation, and the wisdom that you've worked so hard to gather, and find ways to apply it that will help bring your brothers and sisters out of darkness and into God's glorious light. Whenever you share something you've learned from your Bible study, let the love of Jesus Christ always be what motivates you, and never worry about who is impressed.

Our fellowship with the Father is through prayer in the name of Jesus (John 16:23-24). Our fellowship with the Holy Spirit is constant, as He was sent to the Earth on the day of Pentecost, and He will never leave us or forsake us (John 14:16; Acts 2:1-4). What about our fellowship with God the Son, the Lord Jesus Christ?

And the Word became flesh and dwelt among us, and we have seen his glory, glory as of the only Son from the Father, full of grace and truth. - John 1:14

Jesus was the Word made flesh. Our fellowship with the Son is found when we fellowship with His holy, written, living Word in our devotional time and in our Bible study.

You have all the information you need to get started on your path as a Bible student. The only thing that remains is for you to take action and begin applying these steps in your everyday Bible study.

Now that you know *How To Study Your Bible*, it's time for you to start mining your own treasures out of the Word of God. I'm so excited for you! My expectation is that you will enjoy your Bible like never before and that God will increase you spiritually beyond all that you can ask or think!

Closing Prayer

Heavenly Father, I thank You for the grace you've given me to write this book. You know how the enemy fought this effort, but You have brought me the victory, and for that I praise You and give You all of the glory.

I pray that I've been able to bring forth this material to the readers the way You wanted it brought forth, emphasizing the things that You want emphasized. I ask that any mistakes or errors on my part would be overshadowed by the teaching ministry of the Holy Spirit.

For those who have read *How To Study Your Bible*, I pray that the revelations they've gained won't be just information and data in their heads, but revelation that they will act on as they begin to become disciplined in the practices of devotional Bible reading and Bible study.

I pray that You help them be consistent, and to faithfully apply the Bible study methods given in this book, with humility. Guide them in their studies by Your Holy Spirit.

Finally, dear Father, I pray that all who have read this book will be able to take the skills they've learned and use them to draw closer to You.

In the mighty Name of the Lord Jesus Christ I pray,

Amen.

Appendix A

List of Bible Study Tools and Methods

This is a quick reference listing of all the Bible study tools and Bible study methods contained in this book.

Bible Study Tools

Bible Study Methods

Appendix B

The Integrity of God's Word

Everything was created by the Word of God (Hebrews 11:3), and it's by the Word of God that all of creation is held together (Colossians 1:17). We can rely on the Word of God 100% of the time because God never lies. He keeps His Word, and if He says something about any subject, you know whatever He says is true. Believing God's Word simply means you trust in His integrity. Reading over these Bible verses will help you to trust in God and His Word in a greater way, increasing your faith and encouraging your heart.

God is not man, that he should lie, or a son of man, that he should change his mind. Has he said, and will he not do it? Or has he spoken, and will he not fulfill it? - Numbers 23:19

And also the Strength of Israel will not lie nor repent: for he is not a man, that he should repent. - 1 Samuel 15:29 (KJV)

Blessed be the LORD who has given rest to his people Israel, according to all that he promised. Not one word has failed of all his good promise, which he spoke by Moses his servant. - 1 Kings 8:56

The words of the LORD are pure words, like silver refined in a furnace on the ground, purified seven times. You, O LORD, will keep them; you will guard us from this generation forever. - Psalms 12:6, 7

As for God, his way is perfect: the word of the LORD is tried: he is a buckler to all those that trust in him. - Psalm 18:30 (KJV)

The law of his God is in his heart; his steps do not slip. - Psalm 37:31

I will not violate my covenant or alter the word that went forth from my lips. - Psalm 89:34

Forever, O LORD, Your word is settled in heaven. - Psalm 119:89 (NAS)

There are many devices in a man's heart; nevertheless the counsel of the LORD, that shall stand. - Proverbs 19:21 (KJV)

Every word of God proves true; he is a shield to those who take refuge in him. - Proverbs 30:5

The grass withers, the flower fades, but the word of our God will stand forever. - Isaiah 40:8

"This is like the days of Noah to me: as I swore that the waters of Noah should no more go over the earth, so I have sworn that I will not be angry with you, and will not rebuke you. For the mountains may depart and the hills be removed, but my steadfast love shall not depart from you, and my covenant of peace shall not be removed," says the LORD, who has compassion on you. - Isaiah 54:9, 10

So shall my word be that goes out from my mouth; it

shall not return to me empty, but it shall accomplish that which I purpose, and shall succeed in the thing for which I sent it. - Isaiah 55:11

Then the LORD said to me, "You have seen well, for I am watching over my word to perform it."
 - Jeremiah 1:12

I am the LORD. I have spoken; it shall come to pass; I will do it. I will not go back; I will not spare; I will not relent; according to your ways and your deeds you will be judged, declares the Lord GOD.
 - Ezekiel 24:14

For I the LORD do not change; therefore you, Oh children of Jacob, are not consumed. - Malachi 3:6

For truly, I say to you, until heaven and earth pass away, not an iota, not a dot, will pass from the Law until all is accomplished. - Matthew 5:18

Heaven and earth will pass away, but my words will not pass away. - Mark 13:31

But it is easier for heaven and earth to pass away than for one dot of the Law to become void. - Luke 16:17

By no means! Let God be true though every one were a liar, as it is written, "That you may be justified in your words, and prevail when you are judged."
 - Romans 3:4

For all the promises of God in him are yea, and in

him Amen, unto the glory of God by us.
 - 2 Corinthians 1:20 (KJV)

If we are faithless, he remains faithful - for he cannot deny himself. - 2 Timothy 2:13

In hope of eternal life, which God, who never lies, promised before the ages began - Titus 1:2

So when God desired to show more convincingly to the heirs of the promise the unchangeable character of his purpose, he guaranteed it with an oath, so that by two unchangeable things, in which it is impossible for God to lie, we who have fled for refuge might have strong encouragement to hold fast to the hope set before us. - Hebrews 6:17, 18

Jesus Christ the same yesterday, and to day, and for ever. - Hebrews 13:8 (KJV)

Every good gift and every perfect gift is from above, and cometh down from the Father of lights, with whom is no variableness, neither shadow of turning.
 - James 1:17 (KJV)

But the word of the Lord remains forever." And this word is the good news that was preached to you.
 - 1 Peter 1:25

Appendix C

Influences of the King James Bible on the English Language

The 1611 King James Bible has had a massive impact on the English language over the past 400 years. Hearing that is one thing, but when you see so many examples together all at once, it will really hit you how influential the King James Version has been. Here are some examples:

A bird in the hand is worth two in the bush
A broken heart
A cross to bear
A drop in the bucket
A fly in the ointment
A graven image
A house divided against itself cannot stand
A labor of love
A law unto themselves
A man after his own heart
A multitude of sins
A nest of vipers
A peace offering
A person is known by the company he keeps
A stumbling block
A thief in the night
A two-edged sword
A voice crying in the wilderness
A wolf in sheep's clothing
All these things must come to pass
All things to all men

Am I my brother's keeper?
An eye for an eye, a tooth for a tooth
And the word was made flesh
As old as Methuselah
As old as the hills
As white as snow
Ashes to ashes, dust to dust
At my wit's end
Baptism of fire
Be fruitful and multiply
Bite the dust
Blessed are the peacemakers
Blind leading the blind
Born again
Bottomless pit
Breath of life
By the skin of his teeth
By the sweat of your brow
By their fruits ye shall know them
Can a leopard change its spots?
Cast the first stone
Cast your bread upon the waters
Charity begins at home
Coat of many colors
Crumbs which fall from the table
Death, where is your sting
Den of thieves
Don't cast your pearls before swine
Don't let your left hand know what the right
        hand is doing
Drop in the bucket

Dust of the earth
Eat the fat of the land
Eat, drink and be merry
Eye for an eye
Faith will move mountains
Fall by the way side
Fallen from grace
False prophets
Feet of clay
Fell flat on his face
Fell on rocky ground
Fight the good fight
Fire and brimstone
Flesh and blood
Forbidden fruit
Forgive them for they know not what they do
From strength to strength
Gird your loins
Give up the ghost
Go the extra mile
God forbid
Golden calf
Good Samaritan
Hammer swords into plowshares
Handwriting on the wall
Harden your heart
He who lives by the sword, dies by the sword
Holier than thou
How are the mighty fallen
In the beginning was the word
In the twinkling of an eye

It's better to give than to receive
Kill the fatted calf
Labor of love
Lamb to the slaughter
Led as a sheep to the slaughter
Let he who is without sin cast the first stone
Let my people go
Let not the sun go down on your wrath
Let there be light
       Love covers a multitude of sins
Love thy neighbor as thyself
Man shall not live by bread alone
Manna from Heaven
Many are called but few are chosen
Milk and honey
Money is the root of all evil
More blessed to give than to receive
My brother's keeper
My cup runneth over
My heart's desire
My name is legion
New wine into old bottles
No rest for the wicked
No room at the inn
O ye, of little faith
Out of the mouths of babes
Peace offering
Pearls before swine
Physician heal thyself
Pride goes before a fall
Put the words in her mouth

Put your house in order
Reap the whirlwind
Red sky at morning
Scapegoat
See eye to eye
Seek and ye shall find
Set your teeth on edge
Signs of the times
Soft answer turns away wrath
Sour grapes
Spare the rod and spoil the child
Stood by the stuff
Suffer fools gladly
Sufficient unto the day
Swords into ploughshares
Take root
Tender mercies
The apple of his eye
The bread of life
The breath of life
The ends of the earth
The fruits of your loins
The last shall be first
The letter of the law
The lost sheep
The love of money is the root of all evil
The patience of Job
The powers that be
The root of the matter
The salt of the earth
The spirit is willing but the flesh is weak

The straight and narrow
The truth shall make you free
The wages of sin is death
The way of all flesh
The wisdom of Solomon
There's nothing new under the sun
They know not what they do
This too shall pass
Thorn in the flesh
Thou shalt not bear false witness
Thou shalt not kill
Three score and ten
To everything there is a season
To the ends of the earth
Turn the other cheek
Turned the world upside down
Two are better than one
Two-edged sword
Vengeance is mine
Wandering stars
Wars and rumors of wars
Wash your hands of the matter
Weighed in the balance and found wanting
What God has joined together let no man
        put asunder
What is truth?
Wheels within wheels
Where there is no vision the people perish
White as snow
Woe is me
You shall reap what you sow

Scripture Index

How Can I Be Saved?

Are you ready to accept the gift of eternal life that Jesus is offering you right now? If you sincerely desire to receive Jesus into your heart as your Lord and Savior, then here's a suggested prayer you can pray. You don't have to use these exact words. What's most important is that you're talking to God from your heart:

> *"Lord Jesus, I know that I am a sinner and I do not deserve eternal life. But, I believe You died and rose from the grave to make me a new creation and to prepare me to dwell in your presence forever. Jesus, come into my life, take control of my life, forgive my sins and save me. I am now placing my trust in You alone for my salvation and I accept your free gift of eternal life."*

Congratulations! You've just been adopted into the family of God. According to Jesus, all of Heaven is rejoicing:

Just so, I tell you, there is joy before the angels of God over one sinner who repents. – Luke 15:10

You are now at the beginning of a long, exciting, spiritual journey toward a close, intimate relationship with God.

If you've prayed this prayer for the first time, please contact me at *praisereport@michaeldorseyonline.org* so we can celebrate with you!

About the Author

Saved at the age of 10 and Spirit-filled at age 16, Rev. Michael Dorsey has been a Christian for more than 30 years, and a teacher of the Word of God for over 20 of those years. He has ministered to new believers one-on-one, taught various Bible courses, and has been a speaker at various revival meetings and ministers' conferences.

Michael is the author of several books, including the multi-volume *How To Live* series. He has been called by God to help true seekers find Christ, to build up and strengthen new believers, and to train up mature Christians for more effective service.

His passion is discipling new believers, teaching them the Word of God so they can master the circumstances of their lives and be transformed from victims into victors, and then equipping those believers to begin discipling others to the glory of God.

Michael and his wife Katherine, along with their children Robbie and Kirsten, are active partners with Riverside Church in the Baltimore area, where they work in the ministry and assist their Pastor to bless God's people.

THANK YOU!

I really hope you've enjoyed this book, *How To Study Your Bible*, the first volume in the *How To Live* series. Now you're ready to take your life in the Word to the next level of glory in Christ Jesus!

As a personal thank you for reading *How To Study Your Bible*, I'd like to invite you to go to

biblestudy.michaeldorseyonline.com

where you will find additional free resources available for you to download that will further assist you in your daily Christian life.

If you don't yet have your copy of the companion volume to this book, the *Sword Drills: Bible Exercises for the Spiritual Warrior,* I encourage you to get your copy now. You can find out more at:

biblestudy.michaeldorseyonline.com

Once again, thank you so much for your support and your prayers!

Michael Dorsey

How To Study Your Bible

Mining the Treasures of God's Word

is a publication of

MALAKIM
P R E S S

*For further information on
the How To Live series,
along with details of other
publications and upcoming projects
designed to equip Christians
to live victoriously,
please visit us at:*

www.malakimpress.com

www.ingramcontent.com/pod-product-compliance
Lightning Source LLC
Chambersburg PA
CBHW070343090426
42733CB00009B/1271